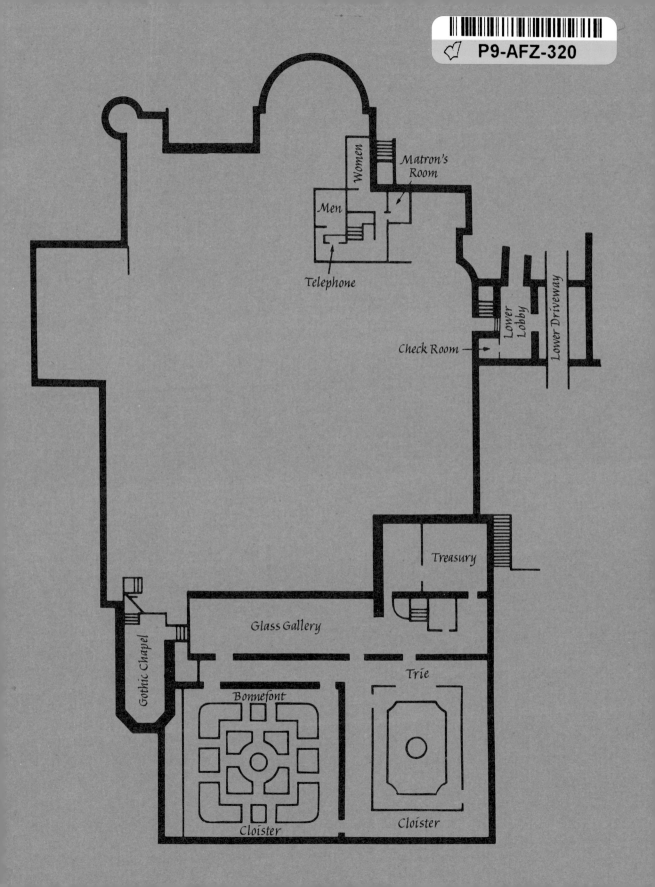

A WALK THROUGH THE CLOISTERS

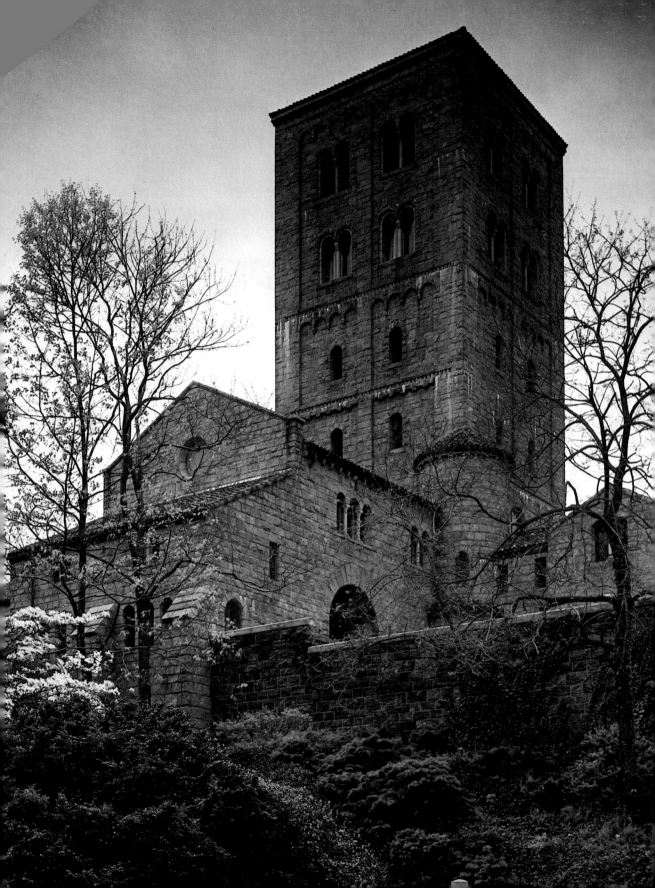

A WALK THROUGH THE CLOISTERS

Text by Bonnie Young
Photographs by Malcolm Varon

THE METROPOLITAN
MUSEUM OF ART
NEW YORK

Distributed by THE VIKING PRESS

FRONTISPIECE: *The Cloisters from the east, showing the tower and ramparts*

Printed in Italy

Copyright © 1979 by The Metropolitan Museum of Art

LIBRARY OF CONGRESS CATALOGING IN PUBLICATION DATA

Young, Bonnie, 1919–
   A walk through the Cloisters.

   "The text is based primarily on various editions of The Cloisters: the building and the collection of medieval art in Fort Tryon Park, by James J. Rorimer."
   1. New York (City). Metropolitan Museum of Art. Cloisters. I. Varon, Malcolm. II. Title.

N611.C6Y68   709'.02'07401471   79-15638
ISBN 0-87099-203-1
ISBN 0-87099-205-8 pbk.   ISBN 0-670-74922-2 (VP)

CONTENTS

INTRODUCTION TO THE CLOISTERS

The Middle Ages—the long moment of Christian history from the time of Constantine (311–337) to the beginnings of the Renaissance—lives for us most vividly in its monuments of architecture and art. The unique collection of The Cloisters offers a sense of medieval culture that is at once intimate and remote, from delicate illuminated miniatures in prayer books and precious metalwork to monumental works of architecture and sculpture. Through the works of art from many different parts of Europe, The Cloisters collection shows the variety and development of the two principal styles of the late Middle Ages: the Romanesque and the Gothic.

The Romanesque style flourished in the eleventh and twelfth centuries. Its primary characteristics in architecture are the round arch and walls built thick to support barrel vaults, reminiscent of the structures of ancient Rome. The period is also noted for the reappearance of monumental figure sculpture and for the achievement of a unity of sculpture with architecture. Strong, at times severe, the Romanesque style is distinguished by its monumentality and abstraction. It is bold and summary in the delineation of overall form, intricate and energetic in details. Spreading throughout the Continent, it reached its zenith around the middle of the twelfth century.

By this time a new style of architecture had begun in France. Its cradle was the Ile-de-France, and its chief progenitor the gifted Abbot Suger of Saint-Denis, minister to Louis VI (reigned 1108–1137) and regent while Louis VII (reigned 1137–1180) was absent on the Second Crusade. Unlike the Romanesque, with its heavy walls and closed dark interiors, the Gothic building, with its pointed arches and the complicated system of thrust and counterthrust that supports its vaulting, gives the effect of an open framework, illuminated by great windows of stained glass. In this period sculpture and ornament began to free themselves from the confines of architectural form. Figures on façades, doorways, and capitals began to move upward and outward, away from the surface. In the thirteenth century, the High Gothic period, the austerity of the late Romanesque was mingled with the transcendental mysticism of the Gothic. The fourteenth century saw an increasing desire for elegance, sophistication, and the mundane, which reached its climax in the late Gothic of the fifteenth century.

Of the great cathedral building of the Middle Ages The Cloisters gives but a suggestion; it is patterned on its more private counterpart, the monastery. Unlike Antonian monasticism, which emphasizes ascetic isolation of the individual, Benedictine monasticism, initiated by Saint Benedict of Nursia (about 480–543), promoted the cenobium, the community. The foundation of the Benedictine abbey of Cluny in 910 marked the establishment of the most important of the great monastic orders of the Middle Ages. At the height of its power in the twelfth century, the Cluniac order controlled more than three hundred monasteries, in France, Italy, Germany, and Spain.

From about 1125 to 1225 the Cistercian order, founded at the abbey of Cîteaux in 1098, established reforms and assumed leadership of European monasticism; its intention was to follow strictly and literally the Rule of Saint Benedict. The Cistercians granted dependent monasteries greater freedom in the management of their own affairs than the Cluniac order, but required the abbots to assemble once a year. In art the Cistercians forbade the depiction of figure and reduced ornament to the simplest types. Toward the end of the thirteenth century monasticism declined, and by the time of the Reformation the institution had already lost much of its great power.

In western European monasteries the most important buildings were grouped around a central cloister, an open court with a covered and arcaded passageway along the sides. The different buildings of the monastery and their disposition followed the requirements of monastic life. Most of the monks' activities, other than those of worship, centered in the cloister. It was there that they walked in meditation, had their school, studied, and sometimes even copied manuscripts. Although formal discussions took place in the chapter house, on occasion the monks were permitted to talk informally in the cloister. The cloisters of western European monasteries were approximately rectangular in shape. They were placed at one side of the church, preferably the south, and usually in the angle formed by the transept and the nave. The chief building on the opposite side was the refectory. The chapter house and sometimes the sacristy and the armarium (library) adjoined the transept. Almost always the cloister side of the chapter house was open, as at Pontaut, although occasionally in colder northern countries it was closed. The dormitory was on a second floor, preferably over the chapter house so that monks could readily reach the church by the night stairs. On the fourth side there were storerooms (the cellarer's quarters) and workshops. Some very large monasteries—for instance, the great Cistercian abbey of Clairvaux—had several cloisters, as numerous buildings were necessary to serve the complex requirements of a large community.

The site of The Cloisters, atop a hill overlooking the Hudson River, may be the closest approximation of a monastic setting possible in an American city: the monks preferred isolated spots, the Benedictines usually on mountaintops, the Cistercians in secluded river valleys. The achievement of the collection and its fine location were the result of the efforts of many skilled and dedicated individuals. The initial imagination was that of the American sculptor George Grey Barnard. Before 1914, when he lived in France, Barnard collected much of the architectural material seen in The Cloisters today, including the columns and capitals of the Saint-Guilhem, Cuxa, Bonnefont, and Trie cloisters.

Barnard's accomplishment in exhibiting this material in a special building on Fort Washington Avenue, not far from The Cloisters' site, was recognized when he put the collection up for sale in the 1920s. A newspaper asked: "Is this gem of French art to be torn from the environment so patiently and lovingly created for it and sold to some more enterprising city?" The reply to that public question came in 1925 when John D. Rockefeller, Jr., donated funds to The Metropolitan Museum of Art for the purchase and continued exhibition of the collection, to which he added some forty medieval sculptures from his own collection. Subsequently, when Rockefeller presented to New York City the land that became Fort Tryon Park, he reserved the northern hilltop for the construction of a larger and better-developed museum of medieval art.

The design for this structure was entrusted to Charles Collens, the architect of the Riverside Church in New York. Collens' first consultant in the planning was Joseph Breck, Assistant Director of the Metropolitan Museum. Upon Breck's death in 1933, the responsibility passed to his colleague James J. Rorimer. Collens and Rorimer, architect and curator, worked closely together throughout the construction period, and more than any others, determined the final form of the building.

4

After four years of construction beginning in 1934, The Cloisters opened in 1938. It is not a copy of any particular medieval structure, but an ensemble of rooms and gardens that suggest, rather than duplicate, the European originals. The rooms and halls and chapels of the main floor are built around the largest of the four cloisters, the one from Saint-Michel-de-Cuxa. On the lower floor, which is served by two stairways, are the Gothic Chapel, the walls of which rise the height of the two floors, and two garden cloisters, the Bonnefont and the Trie. On the lower floor, too, will be found the Glass Gallery and the Treasury, which house objects not closely connected with any of The Cloisters' architectural settings.

ACKNOWLEDGMENT: The text is based primarily on various editions of *The Cloisters: The Building and the Collection of Medieval Art in Fort Tryon Park* by James J. Rorimer. A number of members of the Museum staff, past as well as present, have indirectly contributed through additional research and publications on The Cloisters collection. Leon Wilson, editor of the book, wrote the Unicorn Tapestries chapter and has been of inestimable help throughout the preparation of the text. Unpublished material on the tombs of the counts of Urgel was supplied by Timothy B. Husband, Administrator of The Cloisters.

B.Y.

THE ROMANESQUE HALL

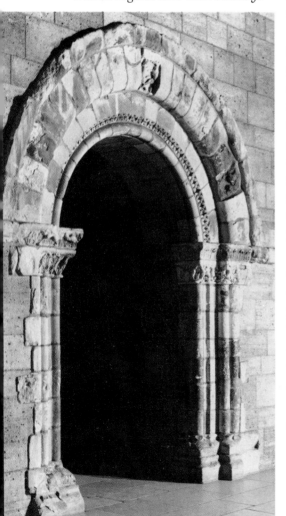

The Entrance Door, Romanesque in style. French, possibly from the Poitou region. Mid-12th century.

Incorporated in the Romanesque Hall, the first room usually entered by The Cloisters' visitor, are three examples of a crucially important feature of Christian architecture: the entrance to the church. Extolled as the "gate of heaven," the "portal of glory," and the "triumphal gate," the entranceway had developed by the eleventh to twelfth centuries from the simple style of early Christian times to the more adorned but still austere mode of the Romanesque. These three doors show the evolution of medieval architecture, from the Romanesque to the Gothic.

The Entrance Door, which dates from about 1150, is a typical example of Romanesque style. The monumental proportions of the round arch impart a sense of grandeur and weight, and the decoration, sparse though it is, reinforces the impression by emphasizing the keystone and capitals. On the keystone two animals on their hind legs, one probably a boar, confront one another; the capitals are carved with acanthus leaves, birds, and animals, both real and imaginary. Although it is no longer known where this doorway once stood, it has similarities to portals and windows of churches in the Poitou region, in west central France.

Representing a transitional style between the Romanesque and Gothic is the Reugny Door, salvaged from a crumbling church in Reugny in the upper Loire valley. A principal Gothic feature is the pointed arch, which gives the portal an upward movement that contrasts with the round solidity of the Entrance Door. In the Reugny Door, too, the decoration is more elaborate and more pronounced, the arch is more deeply recessed, the columns

6

and capitals have greater individuality. Originally supporting the arch were two columnar jamb figures, probably of saints, in the Romanesque sculptural style. The distinctive Romanesque details of stylized folds of drapery and downward-pointing feet can be seen on the fragment of the one figure that remains.

In the third door, from the monastery church of Moutiers-Saint-Jean, in Burgundy, the Gothic style has reached its full development, the many separate elements combining to create a harmonious and magnificent whole. In contrast to the formal patterns of Romanesque art, the carving here is naturalistic. The foliage on the capitals and on the trefoil arch over the figures of Christ and the Virgin on the tympanum is delicately worked; the two

Door from a late Romanesque church at Reugny, central France. Late 12th century. Background: the Saint-Guilhem Cloister.

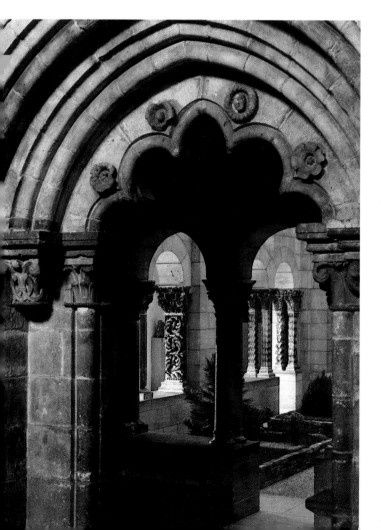

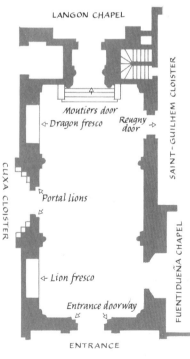

Detail of left-hand figure on Moutiers-Saint-Jean door, possibly of Clovis, first Christian ruler of France.

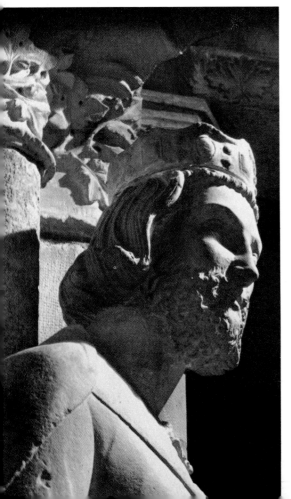

large figures of kings in their canopied niches stand free, no longer acting as supporting columns as did their predecessors at Reugny; and the drapery of all figures, including that of the forerunners of Christ in niches along the sides of the door, falls in realistic folds.

As with most medieval sculpture, the stone was polychromed. Traces of paint still can be seen on the king at the left, on the angels over the door, and on the tympanum, though the paint on the angels may indicate guidelines for work the sculptor had yet to carve.

The two kings were perhaps intended to be David and Solomon, the kings of Judah who were often associated in medieval art with scenes of the coronation of the Virgin. From at least the sixteenth century, however, the figures were thought to represent Clovis, the first Christian ruler of France, and Clothar, his son and successor. The tradition is that Clovis, in the year of his conversion, probably 496, granted the monastery of Moutiers-Saint-Jean a charter that exempted it in perpetuity from both royal and ecclesiastical jurisdictions. The banderoles held by the sculptures may represent the supposed charter of 496 and the confirming charter said to have been granted by Clothar in 539.

Like many other monasteries, Moutiers-Saint-Jean was favored with a long period of noble patronage, and in the thirteenth century, when this entrance was designed, the establishment prospered under the protection of the dukes of Burgundy. The church's fortunes declined with the onset of religious and political upheaval: it was sacked in 1567, 1595, and again in 1629, and during the French Revolution was all but destroyed.

According to an eighteenth-century account, the Huguenots who entered the monastery by a ruse in 1567 "broke the statues of the Saints and Founder Princes." The sculptures of the kings, removed at some time unknown, stood in a private garden in Moutiers, with their heads

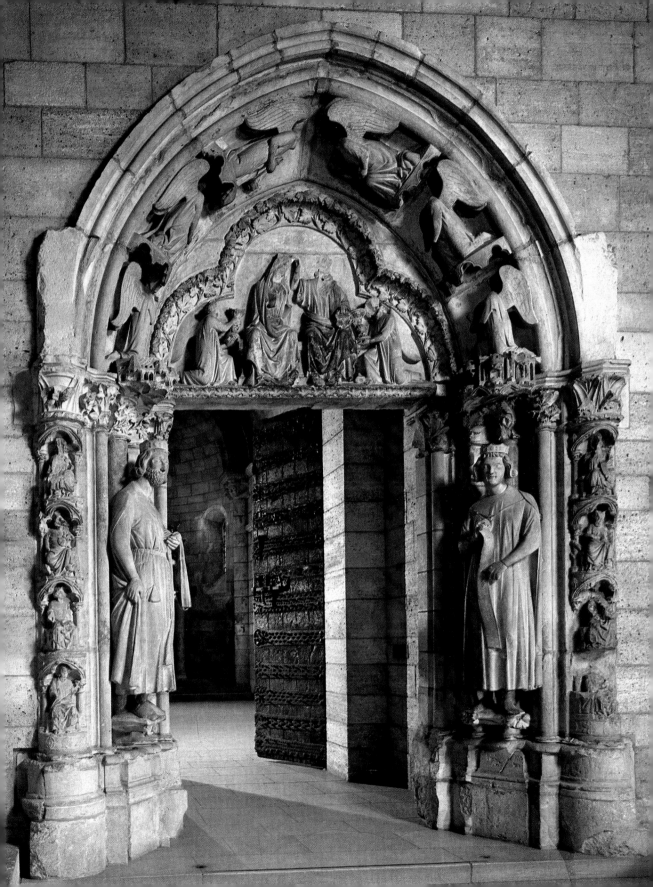

transposed, until 1909. With the heads properly placed, the statues were reunited with the portal in 1940.

Although not itself a medieval monument, the doorway to the Cuxa Cloister is flanked by a pair of medieval sculptures of a kind often to be found guarding the entrances to churches. According to medieval bestiaries, lions are supposed to sleep with their eyes open, and therefore represent paragons of Christian watchfulness. These lion sculptures, of reddish marble, are thought to have come from the entrance to a church in the hamlet of Quattro Castella, near Reggio Emilia, in Italy. One digs his claws into a calf, the other holds down a lamb. Although some sculptured lions were freestanding, this pair shows a flat upper surface with a square hole surrounded by an impressed circle, indicating that they once held columns.

In the wall fresco nearby is another lion, one of a pair that watched over the entrance to the chapter house in the monastery of San Pedro de Arlanza, in northern Spain,

BELOW: *frescoes from the chapter house of the monastery of San Pedro de Arlanza, near Burgos, Spain. About 1220.*

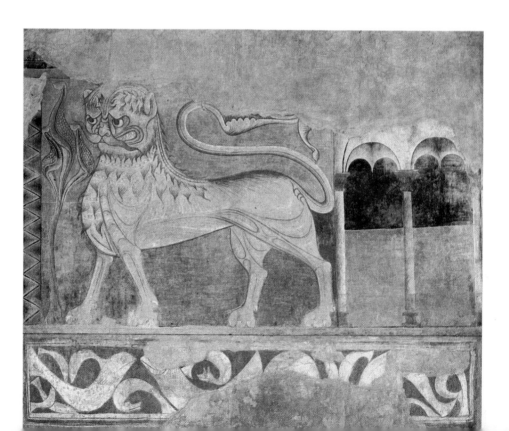

now in ruins. Fierce and Oriental-looking, the Arlanza lion stands between an arcade and a flowering tree—the image of invincible power. In a second fresco from Arlanza a winged dragon soars menacingly across a background of trees. Both paintings are true frescoes, executed while the plaster was fresh, and both are reminiscent, in their freedom of line, of the calligraphy of manuscript illumination. Medieval fresco cycles often looked to illuminations for their models, and these two resemble illuminations in the *Commentary on the Apocalypse* by Beatus of Liebana, a manuscript now in the Pierpont Morgan Library in New York. It was illuminated in a Cistercian convent not far from Arlanza, and the year written in its colophon, 1220, suggests a date for the frescoes.

In the border beneath the dragon are confronted harpies, a fox and goat dancing to music twanged by an ass, and two human figures and two rabbits. It is tempting to read a story into some of this: perhaps Aesop's fable of the ass who found a lyre but had not the skill to play it.

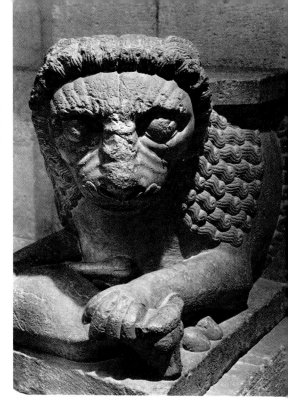

One of a pair of portal lions. North Italian. Early 13th century.

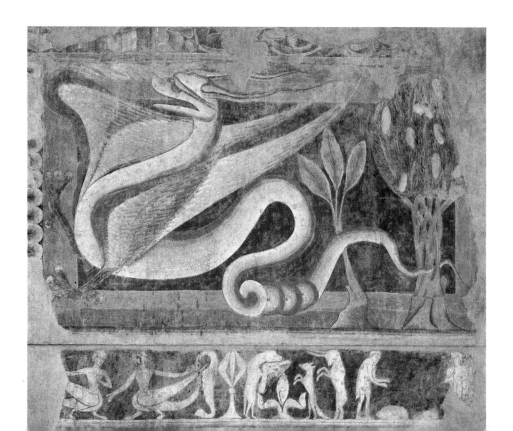

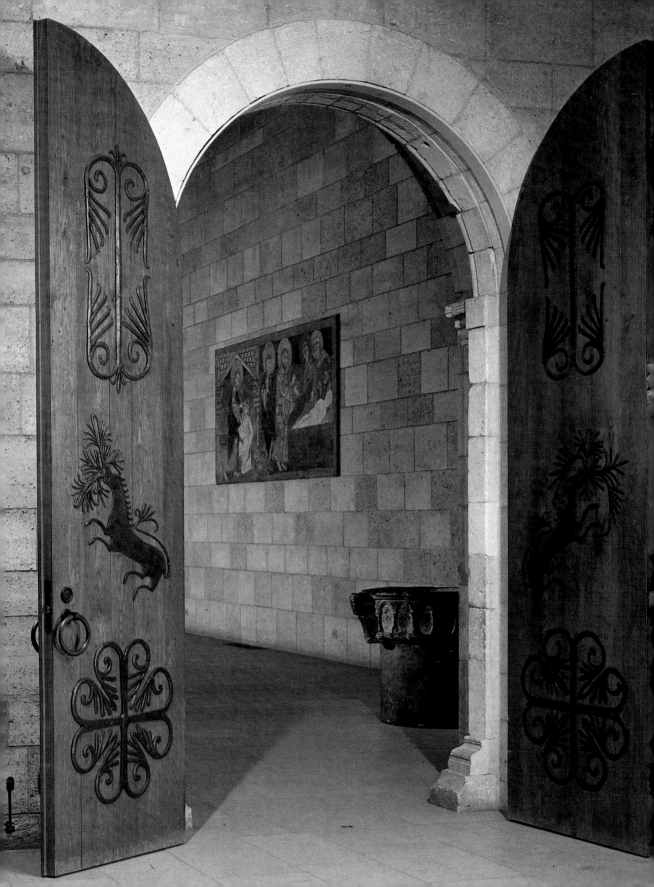

THE FUENTIDUENA CHAPEL

Displayed on the modern oak doors leading from the Romanesque Hall into the Fuentidueña Chapel are handsome wrought-iron mountings from the eleventh or twelfth century. Made for a door of the church of Saint-Léonard-de-Noblac, near Limoges, these decorative works show resemblances to illuminations in two eleventh-century manuscripts created in the monastery of Saint-Martial in Limoges. The leaping animals may have been intended as lions, since they have manes and clawed feet, but may also be examples of the fantastic beasts that held such fascination for medieval artists and craftsmen. Issuing from the animals' mouths are floral sprays, echoed in the tassels at the ends of their tails and repeated in the finials of the scroll-form mounts.

Just inside the entrance is a large baptismal font carved of black calcite, which came from the region near Maastricht and Tongres, where the river Meuse crosses the border between Belgium and the Netherlands. The date of the font, about 1200, is suggested by its decoration: the arcade with small animals supporting the columns, which resembles elements of the twelfth-century Servatius church in Maastricht and the early thirteenth-century cloister at Tongres; and the four projecting human heads with protruding eyes and opulent mustaches, which recall Maastricht sculptures of around the beginning of the thirteenth century.

THE FUENTIDUENA CHAPEL, like the Romanesque Hall, serves for the display of works of medieval art and architecture that once were widely separated. The majestic

OPPOSITE PAGE: *doors with 11th- or 12th-century mountings from church of Saint-Léonard-de-Noblac, near Limoges, France.*

13

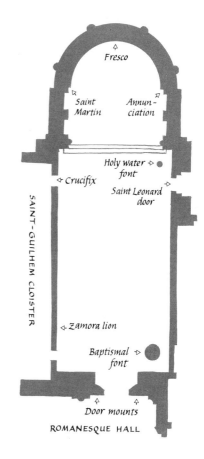

Fresco

Saint Martin   Annunciation

Holy water font

Crucifix

Saint Leonard door

SAINT-GUILHEM CLOISTER

Zamora lion

Baptismal font

Door mounts

ROMANESQUE HALL

Detail of the baptismal font, about 1200.

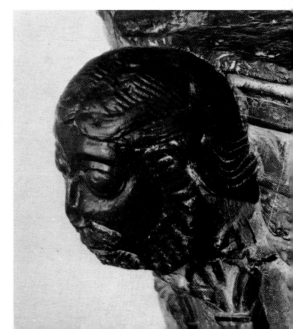

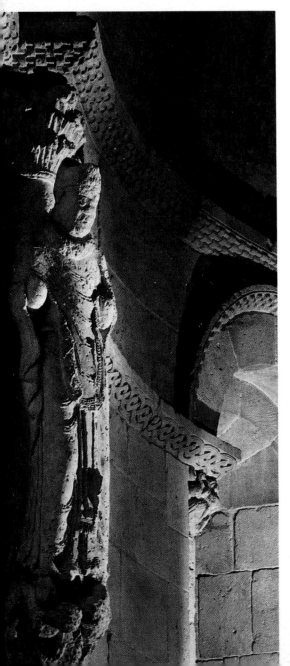

apse came from the church of San Martín in the village of Fuentidueña, about seventy-five miles north of Madrid. According to legend, Saint Martin of Tours, as a gallant young knight, divided his cloak with his sword and gave half of it to a beggar. This charming tale won him many followers during the Middle Ages, and the church at Fuentidueña is one of thousands dedicated to him.

The Romanesque-style church is believed to have been built in the mid-twelfth century, when the fortified town was still of strategic importance to the Christian kings of Castile in their operations against the Moors. No records of the building of the church remain, but, because it stood on a commanding hill not far below a castle, it may have been the castle's chapel. Save for the strongly built apse, the structure itself years ago fell in ruins. In The Cloisters the apse has been placed in a setting that reproduces in part the architectural plan of the original church: as in many Segovian churches there are no side aisles and no transept.

Constructed of some three hundred blocks of golden limestone, the apse begins in a graceful arch, rises to a barrel vault, and culminates in a half dome. Because the windows were not glazed, they were designed to permit maximum light and minimum discomfort from weather, flaring from slits at the outside to splayed jambs at the interior. These small windows and the massive, fortress-like walls contribute to the feeling of austerity that is typical of Romanesque churches.

Honoring Saint Martin is a sculpture that, along with the carving of the Annunciation to the Virgin on the opposite wall, serves as a pier figure in the apse. The two large pieces, of a finer and grayer limestone than the apse itself, may not have been included in the original plan, since sculptures of this size and workmanship—though common on façades—were rarely placed in apses and since the two have no structural function. It may be that they

14

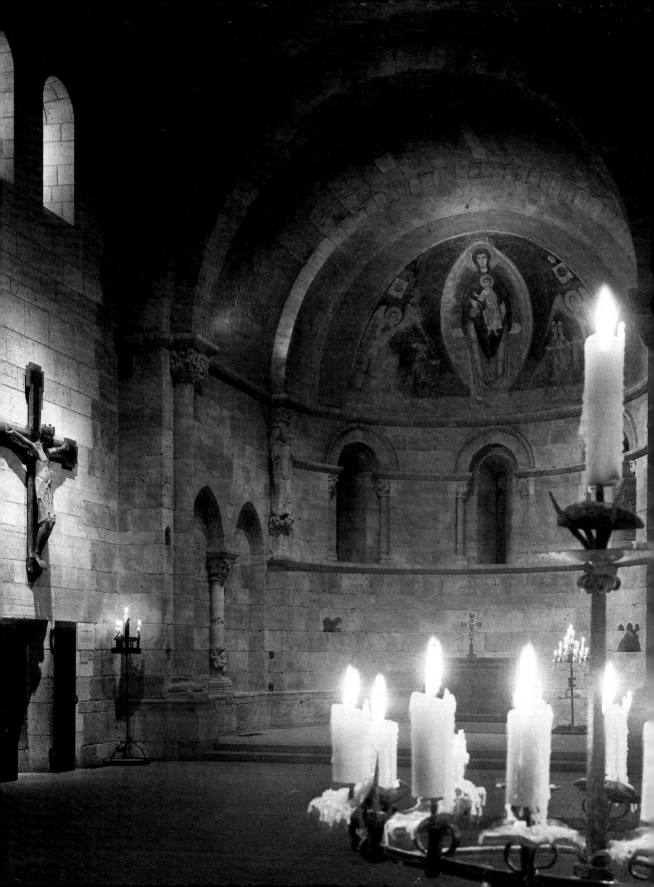

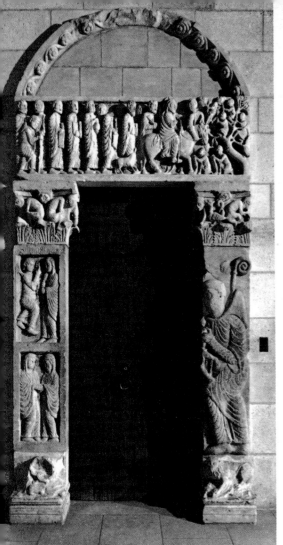

were originally intended to flank a portal, like the kings of the Moutiers-Saint-Jean door in the Romanesque Hall. In any case, the pier figures make a striking contrast in styles. The mannered folds of Saint Martin's drapery give him a formal and static appearance, while the Annunciation scene across the apse seems vigorous and lively, ingeniously carved into a confining space.

The apse contains many other elements of architectural interest. Supporting the arch are capitals that portray, on the left, the Adoration of the Magi, and, on the right, Daniel in the Lions' Den. Fantastic creatures, probably derived from bestiaries rather than from nature, enliven the capitals of the blind arcades and the windows in patterns of dark and light. Further counterpoint is offered by the crisp moldings carved in billet, interlace, and floral patterns, and by the deep, oddly shaped niches in the side walls, which probably held liturgical implements used in the Mass.

In the dome is a fresco from the apse of another Spanish church, San Juan de Tredós, in the Catalonian Pyrenees. Like those in the Romanesque Hall, it is a true fresco, painted onto the wet plaster. Although executed about

Door from the church of San Leonardo al Frigido, Tuscany. About 1175.

To left of door: marble holy water font with Raynerius, patron saint of Pisa, performing miracles. Italian. About 1160.

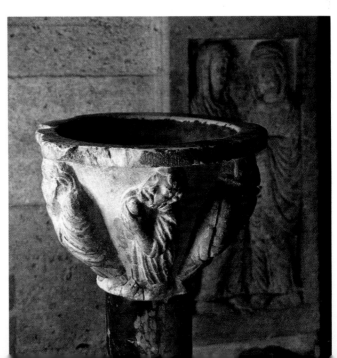

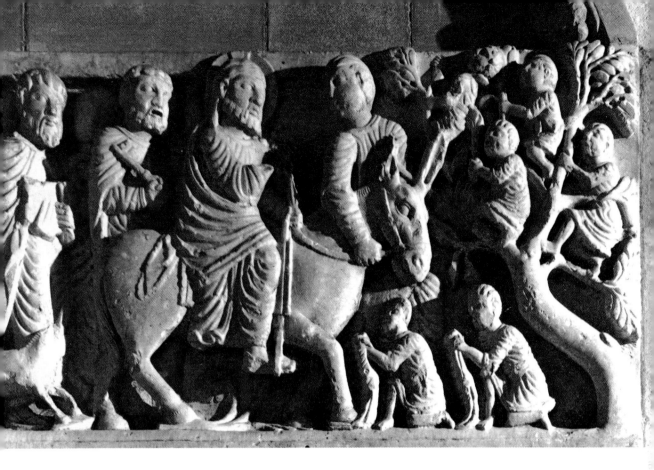

1130–50 in the Romanesque style, it resembles a Byzantine mosaic in the rich play of color, the sophisticated stylization of costume, the jeweled throne, and above all in the interpretation of the Virgin as the Mother of God—severe, remote, and transcendental. On either side of this stern personage are the angels Michael and Gabriel and smaller representations of the Three Wise Men, all labeled and all wearing small hats of the Eastern tradition, rather than the more familiar crowns of Western art.

TO THE RIGHT of the apse is a Romanesque door from the church of San Leonardo al Frigido, a few miles northwest of Massa-Carrara, in Tuscany. The door was described in place in the church in a guidebook of 1879, but by 1893 had been removed to a villa in Nice, and in the

Detail of the lintel from San Leonardo al Frigido: Christ entering Jerusalem.

17

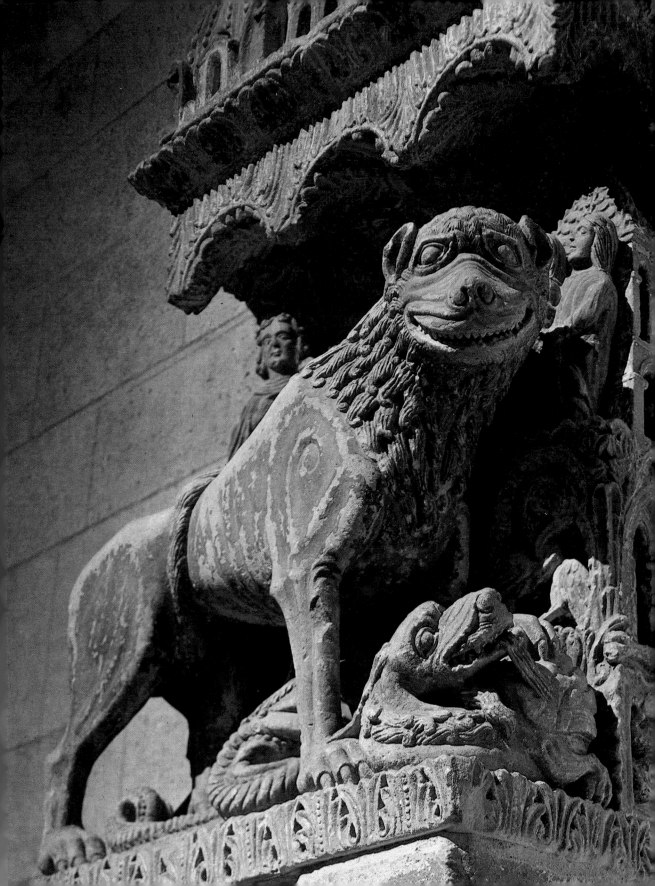

1950s was found lying abandoned in a field near Nice. Saint Leonard of Aquitaine, the patron of the church and of prisoners, is portrayed twice on the door. On the right jamb he carries a shackled prisoner who gazes up at his protector, and on the panel above the opening he accompanies the twelve apostles following Christ into Jerusalem. The treatment of this scene on the lintel undoubtedly follows a representation on an Early Christian sarcophagus, reflecting the revival of interest in late antique and Early Christian art that occurred in Tuscany during the twelfth century. An ancient sarcophagus has served even more directly on the jambs—as the actual material cut lengthwise and reused for the carving. Here, the sculptor has been forced to crowd the scene of saint and small prisoner into the narrow rectangle of the original stone.

On the west wall of the chapel is a Spanish sculpture in which Christ is represented as the Lion of the Tribe of Judah. This thirteenth-century carving and its companion piece, a lioness, once guarded the portal of the

OPPOSITE PAGE: *sculpture from the church of San Leonardo, Zamora, Spain. 13th century. Limestone with polychromy.*

Behind the lion from Zamora, Christ in heaven, crowning the Virgin, with the archangel Gabriel to the left, and Saint Leonard and two prisoners to the right.

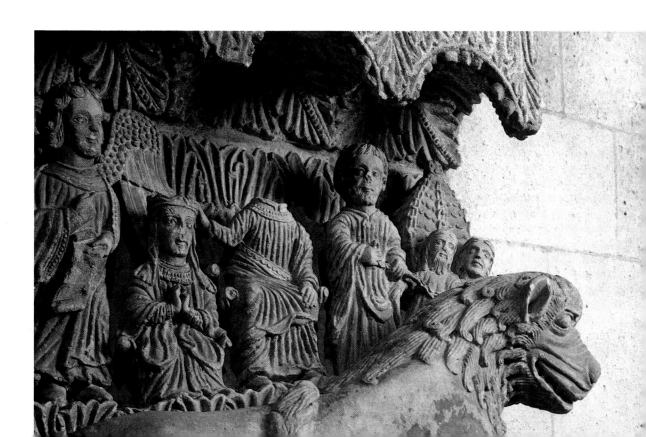

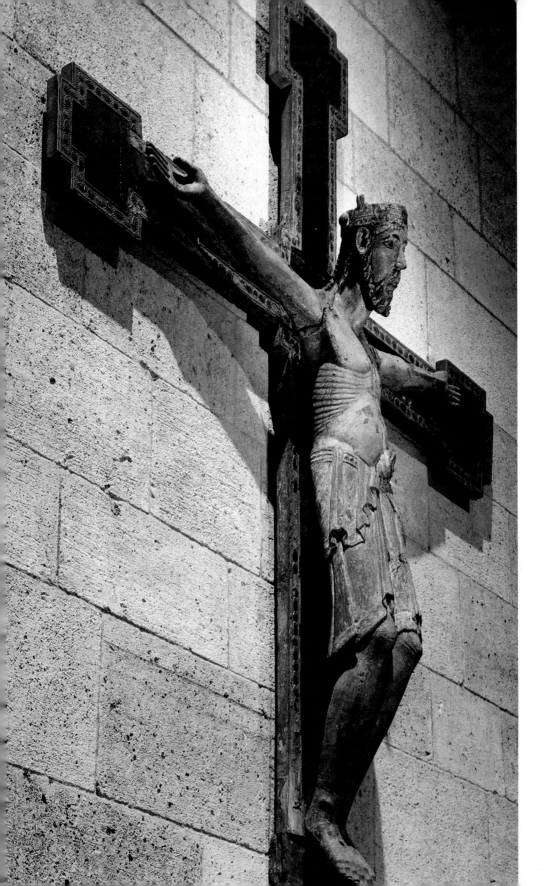

church of San Leonardo in Zamora, northwest of Madrid. Unlike the crouching Italian lions in the Romanesque Hall, this pair was originally set high overhead, on a gable doorway. Trampled under the lion's feet is a serpent, symbol of Satan, and half hidden behind the lion is a scene of Christ crowning the Virgin, attended by the archangel Gabriel and Saint Leonard. Once again Leonard is shown in the service of prisoners, here giving two of them their freedom. The elaborate canopy above the figures was probably inspired by similar architecture in the roof dome of the twelfth-century cathedral in Zamora. A considerable amount of the original polychromy can still be seen on the stone.

The large Spanish crucifix hanging on the wall near the apse is one of the finest surviving examples of the Romanesque type, in which the almost horizontal arms, the symmetrical anatomy, and the flattened folds of the drapery give the figure an impressive dignity. Wearing the golden crown of the King of Heaven as victor over death, this twelfth-century Christ contrasts sharply with crucifixes of later times, in which the figure, wearing the crown of thorns, is shown in the full agony of his suffering. The crucifix is in good condition. The figure, of white oak, and the cross, of pine, retain much of their original paint, and the body is held to the cross by its original iron fastenings. The gesso base over which the paint was applied is thick, and, at some points is even molded to produce finer details than could be achieved by carving. On the ends of the crossbars were probably once painted the figures of Mary and John, and, at the top, the hand of God, the moon and sun, or some other symbol. The letters "INRI" probably filled the space on the upright above Christ's head.

In style, the crucifix is almost identical with an ivory figure of Christ in a reliquary made for Gonzalo Menendez, bishop of Oviedo, 1162–75. There is a tradition that the crucifix once hung behind an eighteenth-century choir screen in the convent of Santa Clara, near Palencia, Spain.

21

Detail of crucifix.

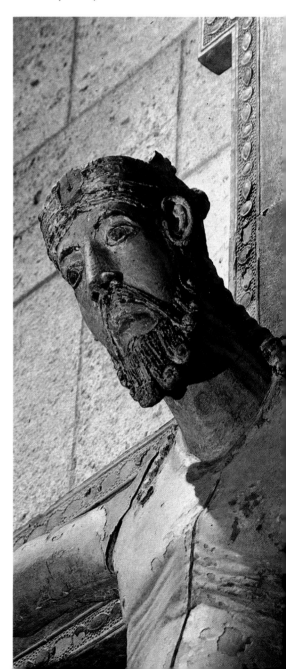

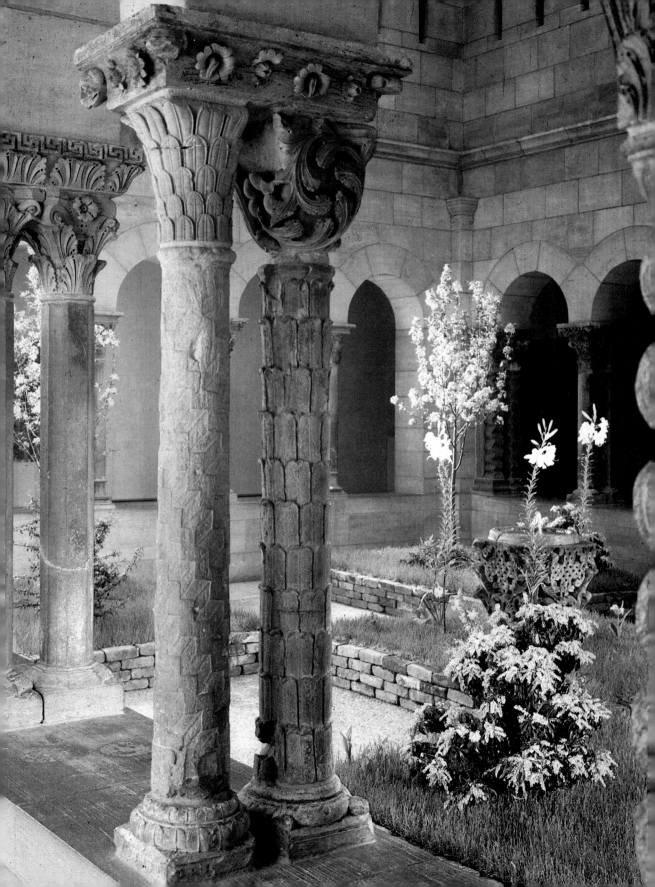

THE SAINT-GUILHEM CLOISTER

Though it is not the oldest, this is usually the first of the four cloisters that one enters during a visit to The Cloisters. The cloister form, a rectangular courtyard with covered, arcaded walks around its four sides, is only partly realized here: the court is smaller than the original and is protected beneath a skylight. Still, Saint-Guilhem retains the standard feature of a garden, in somewhat modified form. Each year, from the Christmas season into spring, shrubs and flowering plants are installed in raised beds in the courtyard.

The Benedictine abbey of Saint-Guilhem-le-Désert was founded in 804. Until the twelfth century it was called Gellone, after the once lonely valley in southern France, near Montpellier, in which it stood. The founder, Guilhem, count of Toulouse and duke of Aquitaine, was one of Charlemagne's paladins. Minstrels, in their *chansons de geste*, told of how Guilhem captured Nîmes by bringing his soldiers within the walls in wine casks; of how he freed Rome from a besieging pagan army but lost the tip of his nose in the battle; of how, when imprisoned by a Saracen king, he escaped with the help of the king's own wife, whom he later married. While much of this is legend, it is known that Guilhem became a monk in the monastery he founded. When he died, the legend continues, the church bells throughout the province rang without any hand on their ropes. Already a hero, Guilhem became a saint, and in the twelfth century the monastery was renamed in the founder's honor. The story of Guilhem had a powerful appeal for medieval pilgrims, who

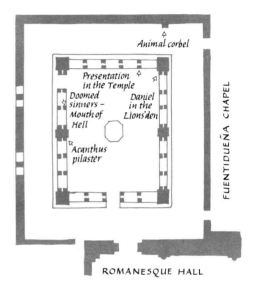

View into Saint-Guilhem Cloister showing indoor garden planted during winter and early spring.

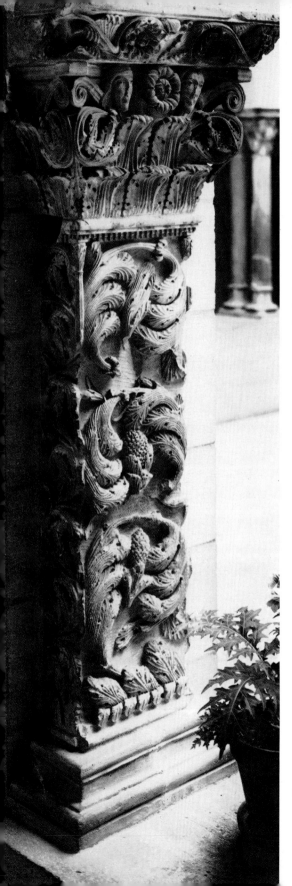

stopped regularly at Saint-Guilhem on their way to Santiago de Compostela in Spain.

With the steady visits of these pilgrims, and the gifts
they brought with them, came a period of prosperity. By
1206 a new cloister had been built at Saint-Guilhem,
incorporating the columns and pilasters seen here. Most
of them are medieval versions of the classical Corinthian
column, based on the spiny leaf of the acanthus. Unlike
their classical models—which could have been any number of classical remains in southern France—the medieval
ornaments show a great variety of design. On a pilaster in
the west arcade is a naturalistic acanthus, complete with
clustered blossoms and detailing as precise as that on gold-
work. Several of the double capitals are treated formally,
stylized much like their classical counterparts. A column
in the east arcade is covered with acanthus leaves in low,
flat relief, while another column is treated as a conven-
tionalized palm tree; beside it is a column with a chevron
pattern (page 22).

Among the most beautiful capitals are those that have
been worked in the drill technique, sometimes in an intricate honeycomb pattern. The drilled dark areas contrast
with the cream-colored limestone and give the foliage a
crisp lacy look that is elegant and sophisticated.

The figural capitals include a Daniel in the Lions' Den,
a Presentation of Christ in the Temple, and a Mouth of

24

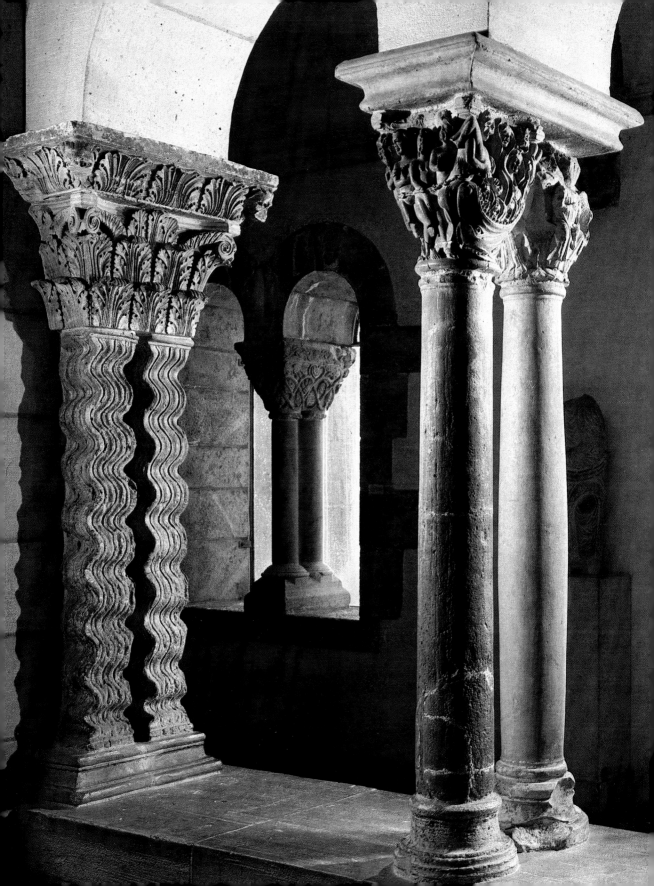

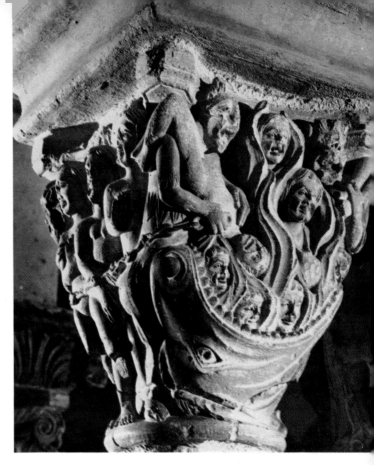

West arcade: capital with sinners hurled into the eternal flames. Gothic style, probably late 12th or early 13th century.

East arcade: capital with stylized acanthus and drillwork.

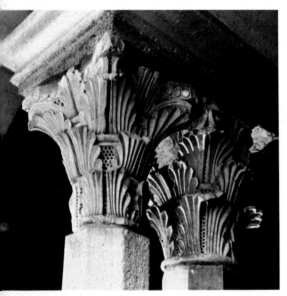

Hell. The Daniel and Presentation carvings are in the Romanesque tradition—flat and stylized—whereas the Hell Mouth with its doomed sinners is in the freer, more realistic Gothic style, with the lively figures beginning to move outward, away from the plane of the stone. The theme of the horrors of hell dominated much of the art—as it did much of the thought—of the Middle Ages. No one doubted the obstinate presence of the Devil and his constant temptations designed to win the sinner's soul. Here, on one side of the Hell Mouth capital, is the face of the Devil; on another, his helpers, who have animal-like body parts and cloven hooves, herd naked sinners in chains to be thrown—on the third side of the capital—into an upturned monster's mouth for the torment of flames.

One of the doomed has a money bag around his neck, a reminder to the living that avarice is a deadly sin.

Some of the Saint-Guilhem abacus blocks, directly above the capitals, show similarly fine details in a variety of imaginative designs. On one, the tendrils of a vine end in human heads; on another, a ribbon meanders in angular folds, suggestive of a Greek fret pattern.

Like other French monasteries, Saint-Guilhem suffered greatly in the religious wars following the Reformation, and it was sold to a stonemason during the Revolution. The damages were so severe that there is now no way of determining the original dimensions of the cloister or the number and sequence of its columns. Those collected here served in the nineteenth century as grape-arbor supports and ornaments in the garden of a justice of the peace in nearby Aniane.

North arcade: two views of capital with Presentation of Christ in the Temple. Joseph kneels, supporting the Child's feet. Mary, behind him, carries a dove. Romanesque style, about 1150.

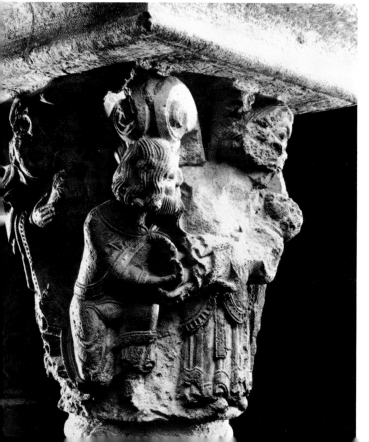

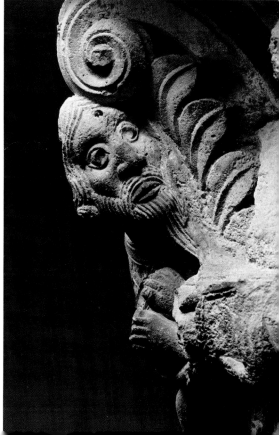

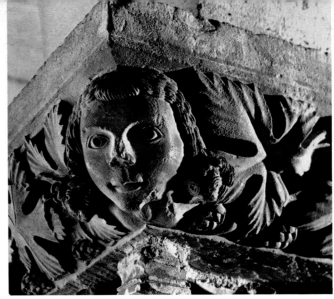

East arcade: masklike head in delicate naturalistic grapevine on an abacus block.

North arcade: one of the corbels from the abbey of Notre-Dame-de-la-Grande-Sauve, near Bordeaux, France. 12th century.

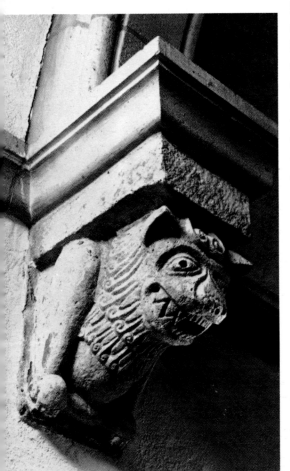

The fountain at the center of the court was once a capital in the church of Saint-Sauveur at Figeac, northwest of Montpellier. In style it is earlier than the Saint-Guilhem carvings, and, since it supported an architectural element high above the floor, its ornamentation—stylized acanthus and interlacing—is more deeply cut than that on the cloister carvings.

Humorous corbels, reminiscent of gargoyles, support the cornice and ribs of the vault over the cloister walks. Of the same period as the Saint-Guilhem carvings, these corbels once supported an exterior cornice at the abbey of Notre-Dame-de-la-Grande-Sauve, near Bordeaux. The handsomely carved capitals in the two windows in the west wall probably also came from La Sauve.

OPPOSITE PAGE:
Fountain made from a capital of the late 11th century, from the church of Saint-Sauveur, Figeac, France, in the center of the courtyard.

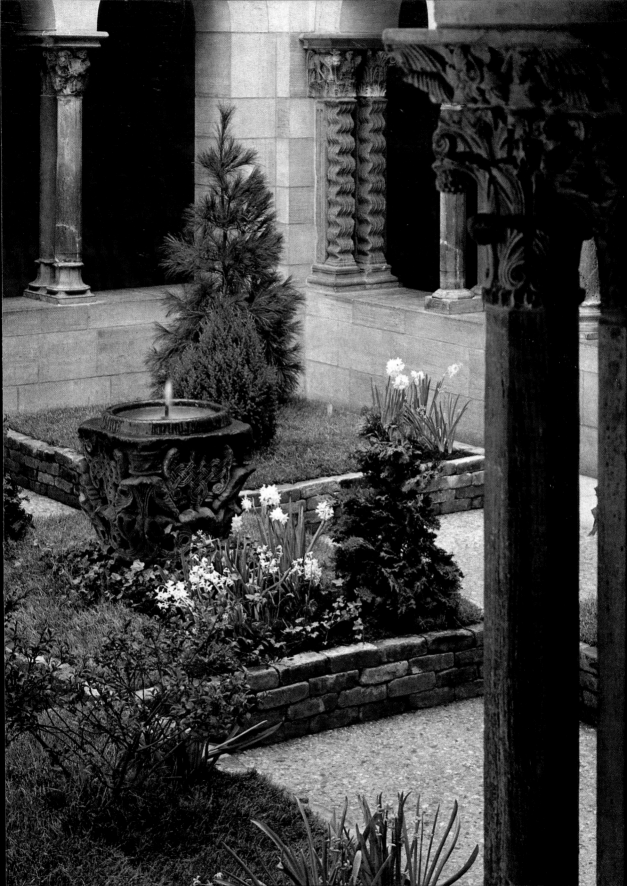

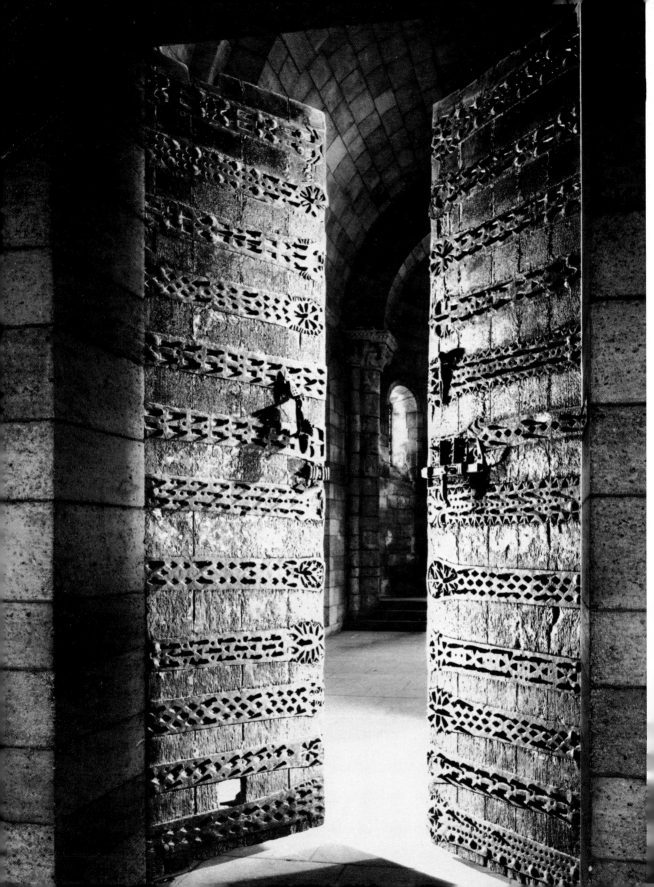

THE LANGON CHAPEL

Entering the Langon Chapel from the Romanesque Hall, the visitor passes through massive oak doors closely bound with ornamental ironwork. Shut and bolted, such doors could withstand all but the heaviest of battering rams, protecting a castle during a siege or saving a church and its treasures from marauders. Because of the hard wear they received, such doors had to be replaced often and, consequently, relatively few are still in existence. This pair is said to have come from the Pyrenees region.

Although the primary purpose of the spiked iron bands was to strengthen the doors, the diversity of their decoration adds considerable visual interest. On one band is a figure of Christ on the cross, set against a wheel pattern; on others are geometric and leaf-form patterns and horses' heads with stylized manes. Although some motifs are repeated, no two bands are exactly alike.

The old stonework of the chapel is from the church of Notre-Dame-du-Bourg, which stood in Langon, southeast of Bordeaux. In 1126, monks of the Benedictine abbey of La-Grande-Sauve, near Bordeaux, were ordered to build at Langon a church to be dedicated to the Virgin. Construction of the church must have been begun well before 1155, since the church had received important gifts by that date. Later—like so many of the buildings whose monuments are now in The Cloisters—Notre-Dame-du-Bourg was beset with misfortunes. In 1374, during the Hundred Years War, Bertrand du Guesclin, the constable of France, made a devastating raid on Langon, which was then held by the English. It may have been after this event that the Romanesque transept of the church was rebuilt in

Iron-bound oak doors. French or Spanish, Pyrenees region. 12th century.

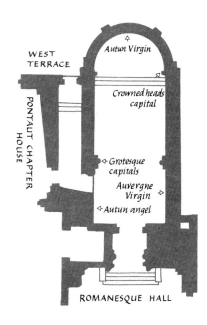

31

A monster and bending half-length figures support the vault on the left side.

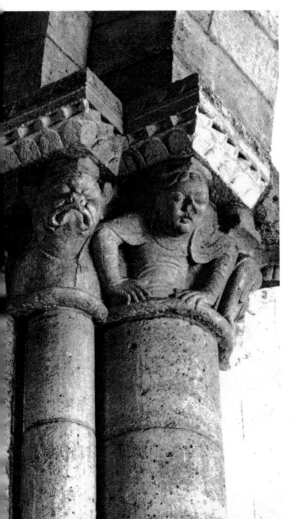

the Gothic style. Then, in 1566 Gabriel de Montgoméry, leading his Huguenot troops, sacked Langon. Undoubtedly he did not spare the church. Although the shell still stands, the capitals seen here, salvaged from the choir, are all that remain of the figural sculpture. The nave was used as a Jacobin meeting room during the Revolution, and more recently parts of the church have served as a dance hall, tobacco warehouse, motion picture theater, and garage.

The simple architectural setting at The Cloisters probably varies little from the original. Based on the rounded arch used by the Romans, the barrel-vaulted ceiling rests on thick walls with small windows—the type of structure needed to support the thrust of the vault. At Langon, the cornice was some 23½ feet above the floor; here it is only 17 feet above, and the original width of the chapel, more than 23 feet, has been decreased proportionately. The reduced dimensions allow the original stonework to dominate over the modern, and they bring the details of the cornice closer to the viewer's eye. The right wall, with its columns, arches, and window, has been installed with little variation from the original Romanesque arrangement. The left wall, reconstructed with modern stonework, incorporates one column complete with its capital, one other large capital, and a smaller one. No traces of what may have been the original painted decorations survive on the brownish white limestone, but touches of paint applied at a later time are still visible.

The capitals do not appear to have a religious significance, nor do they tell a story. The bending half-length figures recall Greek atlantes and caryatids in their ceaseless effort to support the weight above them. Since Henry II of England and his wife, Eleanor of Aquitaine,

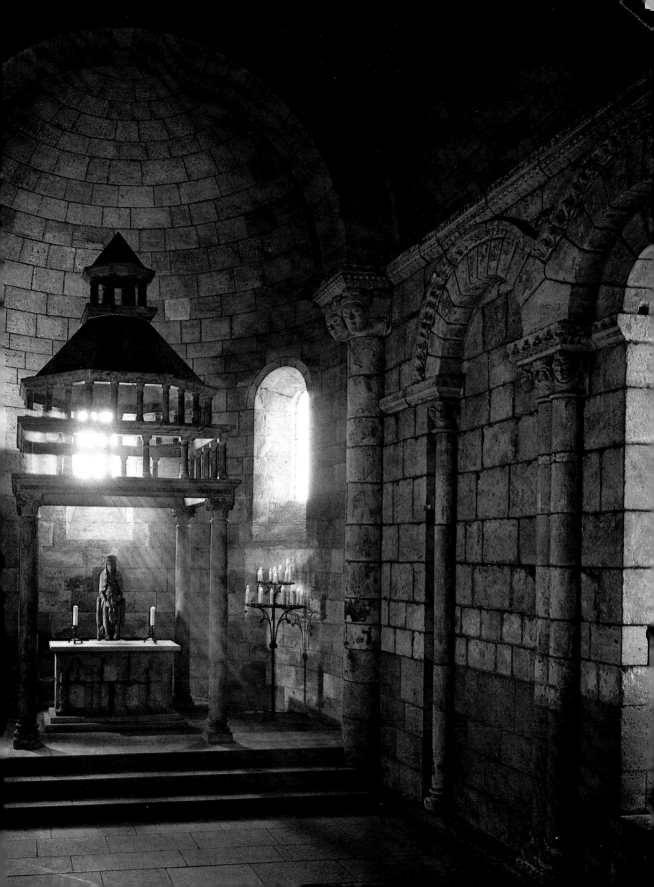

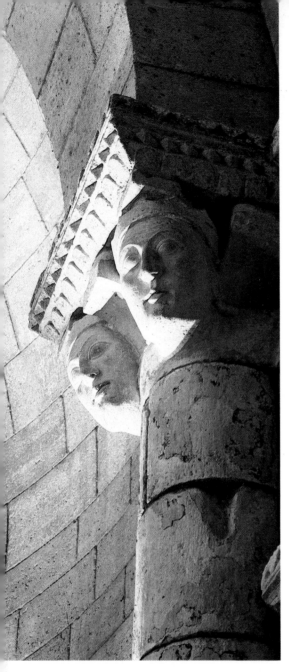

Crowned heads, sometimes thought to represent Eleanor of Aquitaine and Henry II of England, carved on right-hand capital at the juncture of the apse and nave.

are known to have visited the monastery of La-Grande-Sauve in 1155, when the Langon church was still a dependency of the monastery, it is tempting to think that the crowned heads on one of the capitals represent the king and queen, carved possibly to commemorate that occasion. Although the heads cannot be called portraits in any modern sense of the term, they are beautifully carved, with unusual emphasis on simple planes, and, in contrast to other sculptures of the period, they are strikingly life-like. Yet the wish to see these heads as portraying Henry and Eleanor must be tempered with the knowledge that crowned heads in similar style occur in other Romanesque architectural sculpture of the Langon region.

Sheltering the old altar is a tabernacle-like structure of marble with mosaic decorations of colored marble and gilt glass. From this structure, called a ciborium (or baldachin) hung a receptacle that held the consecrated wafer, and in time *ciborium* came to mean the receptacle itself. Until at least 1889 this ciborium was in the church of Santo Stefano, near Fianco Romano, northwest of Rome, in an apse similar in proportion to this one. (The church of Santo Stefano, about which little is known, no longer exists.)

To the right of the entrance to the chapel is a twelfth-century statue of the Virgin and Child enthroned, made in the Auvergne region. Another Virgin and Child enthroned, of the same period, stands behind the altar; it came from Autun, in northeast Burgundy. The differences between these sculptures are as interesting as their similarities. Many such statues were made in France in the twelfth century, when Mary was thought of as "the Throne of the New Solomon, incomparable, sublime, different from all other Thrones." As Mary became the Throne of Wisdom, the child on her lap became Divine

34

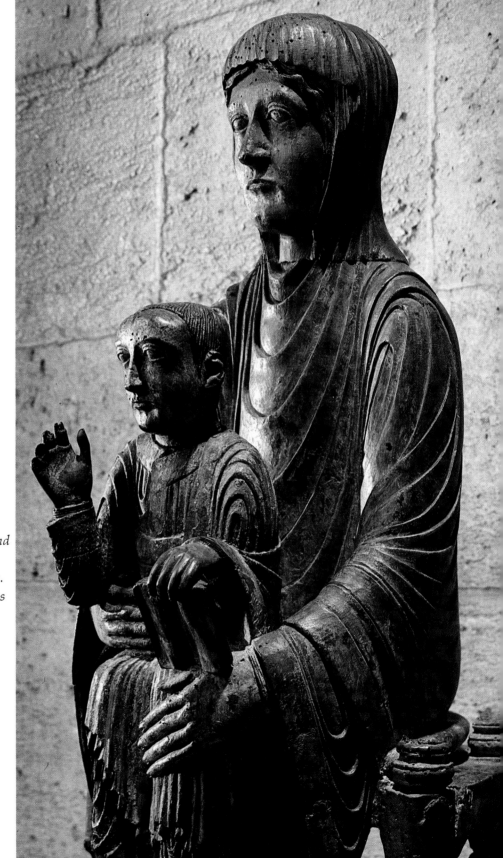

Enthroned Virgin and Child. Auvergne region. 12th century. Walnut with remains of original polychrome painting.

Wisdom. To convey these abstract ideas the statues had to be formal and symmetrical, with a rigid frontality and a stylization both of form and of drapery details. The resulting impression of remote majesty and monumental calm was quite different from the human mother-and-child relationship to be seen in portrayals of the Gothic period, where the child is treated as an infant rather than as the diminutive man he appears to be here.

Both of the chapel's sculptures are of wood, as were most of the French Virgin and Child statues of this type. Examples are either carved from a single block or composed of a number of pieces connected with dowels. The Virgin behind the altar is carved from a single piece of birch, with only the Child's head (now missing) attached by a dowel, and the back hollowed out to discourage cracking or splitting. The statue from the Auvergne was assembled from some eighteen pieces of walnut. While the dowels that once attached the Child's feet are now visible and the Virgin's head is clearly a separate piece set onto the body, the other parts are so cleverly fitted that the joinings are almost imperceptible. Here, the regular and elegant drapery folds fall in an almost lyrical pattern. Still visible in spots on the wood are the remains of the original polychrome coloring, revealing that the hands and faces were once flesh color: the Virgin wore a blue cloak over a red gown, and the Christ Child wore a red mantle over a green garment.

Traces of color can still be seen on the Virgin from Autun as well: her gown and veil were green with a vermilion border and her hair was black. One of the original blue glass inlays for the eyes is still in place. This Virgin is not quite so rigid and frontal as the one from Auvergne. Especially noticeable is her human, compassionate expression. In addition, one of her shoulders is higher than

OPPOSITE PAGE: *enthroned Virgin and Child. Autun, Burgundy. First half of 12th century. Birch with traces of original paint.*

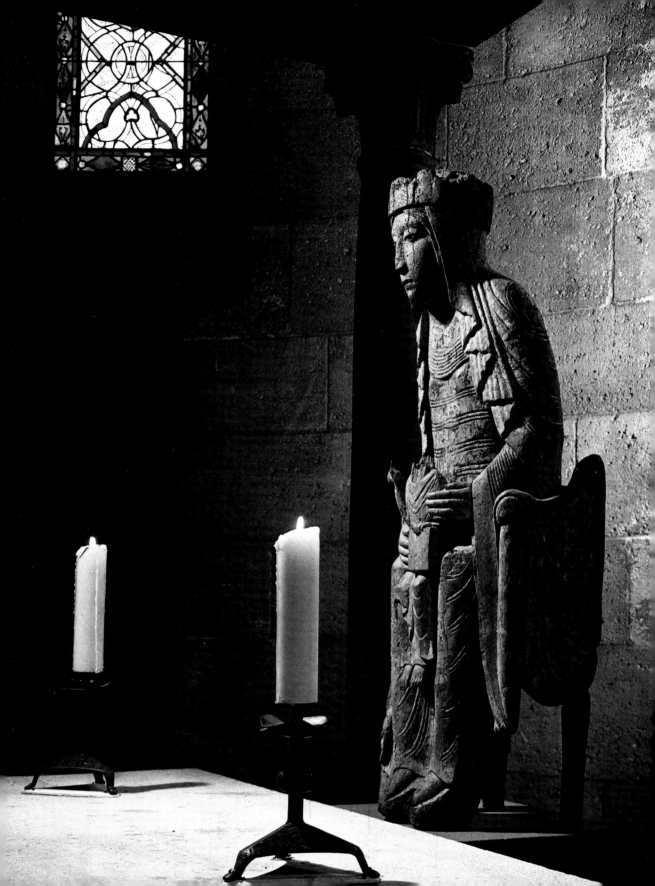

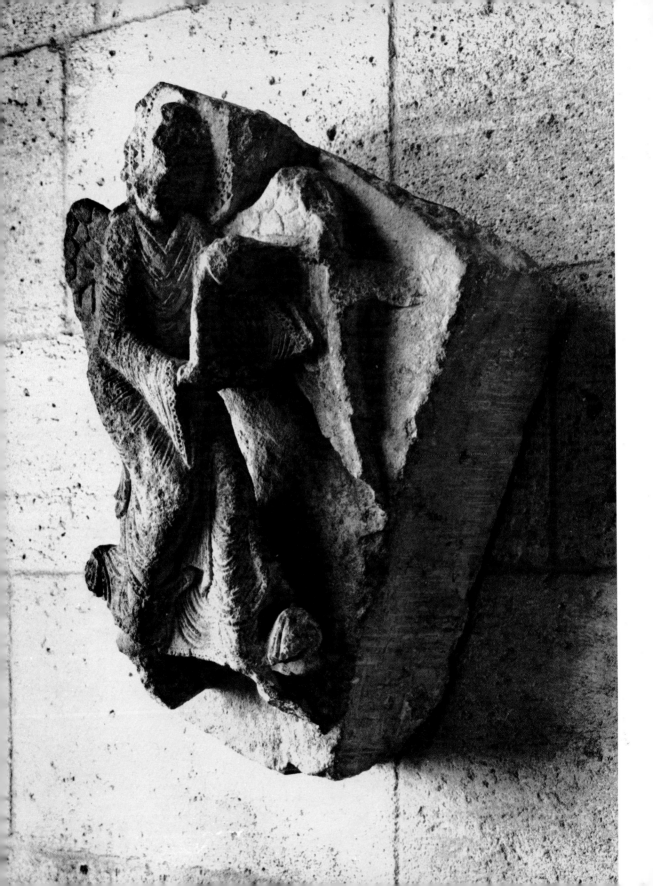

the other, her head is very slightly turned, and the treatment of the drapery suggests movement. The material is portrayed as thin, the folds are indicated by parallel ridges set close together. The upward swirl of the garment at one side, as if blown by a gust of wind, and the face, with its heavy-lidded eyes, straight mouth, and tiny chin, are reminiscent of sculptures on the main portal of the cathedral of Saint-Lazare in Autun, made probably between 1125 and 1135.

On the wall of the chapel is a limestone angel, a block from a side portal of the cathedral of Saint-Lazare that was demolished in 1766. The angel, which has an airy quality that makes it appear to be in flight, displays the kind of swirling hem found on the Autun Virgin. The fluttering drapery, the folds indicated by fine calligraphic lines, the pearl borders, the carefully feathered wings, the elongated proportions, and the deep undercutting of the figure all relate this angel to those in the Last Judgment scenes on the main portal of the Autun cathedral. This portal, one of the finest examples of French Romanesque art still in existence, is signed "Giselbertus Hoc Fecit." The prominent position of the signature suggests not only Giselbertus' pride in his artistry but his contemporaries' recognition of his preeminence among sculptors.

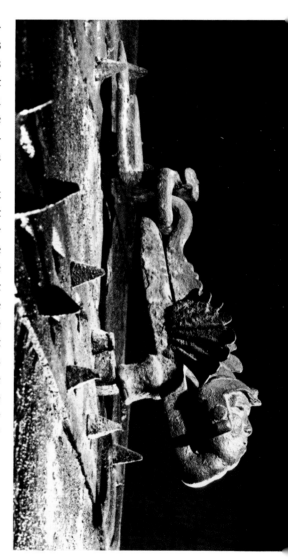

THE PONTAUT CHAPTER HOUSE

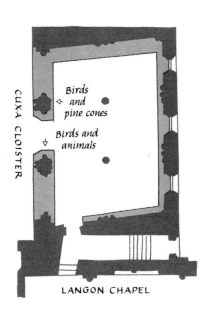

View of the Pontaut Chapter House, showing south wall with courses of brick interrupting the stonework.

The abbey from which the Chapter House came, Notre-Dame-de-Pontaut, in Gascony, south of Bordeaux, was established by the Benedictines about 1115 and in 1151 was given to the Cistercians. Since the Cistercians prohibited sculpture in their churches, one can surmise that the Pontaut Chapter House was built either while the abbey still belonged to the Benedictines or later in the century, when the ban was slightly relaxed.

Each day in such a room the business of the monastery was discussed and a chapter of the order's rule, instructing the monks in every detail of their daily conduct, was read aloud. For these observances, the monks were seated—here, on the stone benches that encircle the room—and the abbot sat on a separate, sometimes raised, seat. The Pontaut abbot's seat may have been placed where a door was opened through the center of the back wall in the nineteenth century to convert the room into a stable. Other relics from that era are iron tethering rings in the two center columns. On the outside wall are three small deep windows that were not glazed; holes in the stone and the remains of hinges show that the openings were once secured with shutters and bars. In the opposite wall, three arches lead to the cloister—here, the Cuxa Cloister—in conformation with the typical layout of Romanesque and early Gothic monasteries. The room offers another look at the transition between Romanesque and Gothic architectural styles: the arches are rounded in the Romanesque manner, but the rib-vaulted ceiling looks forward to the

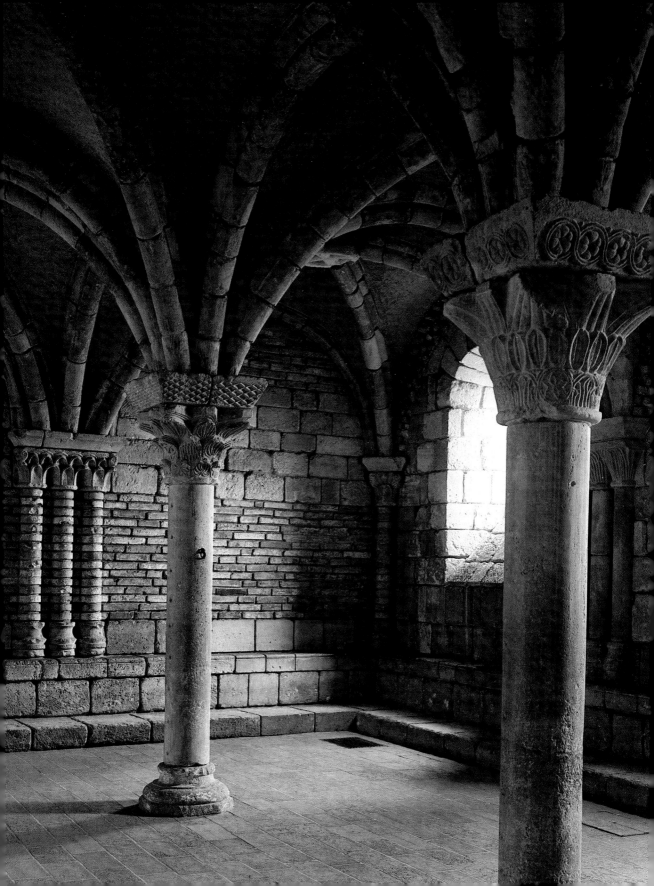

OPPOSITE PAGE: *arched doorway to the chapter house, as seen from the cloister.*

Walk and courtyard of the Cuxa Cloister, seen through the arches of the Pontaut Chapter House.

Gothic. Also as was typical of most monasteries, the monks' dormitory at Pontaut was located directly over the Chapter House.

The Chapter House is one of a few monuments in The Cloisters that is nearly intact. It was brought from its site stone by stone and reconstructed in its slightly irregular plan. Originally the walls were plastered, perhaps even frescoed, and some of the color can still be seen on the ribs of the vaults. (The plaster vaults themselves are

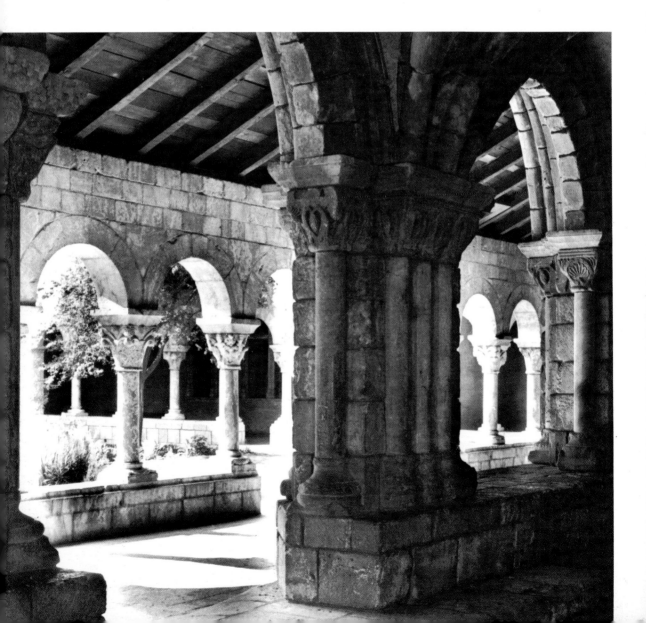

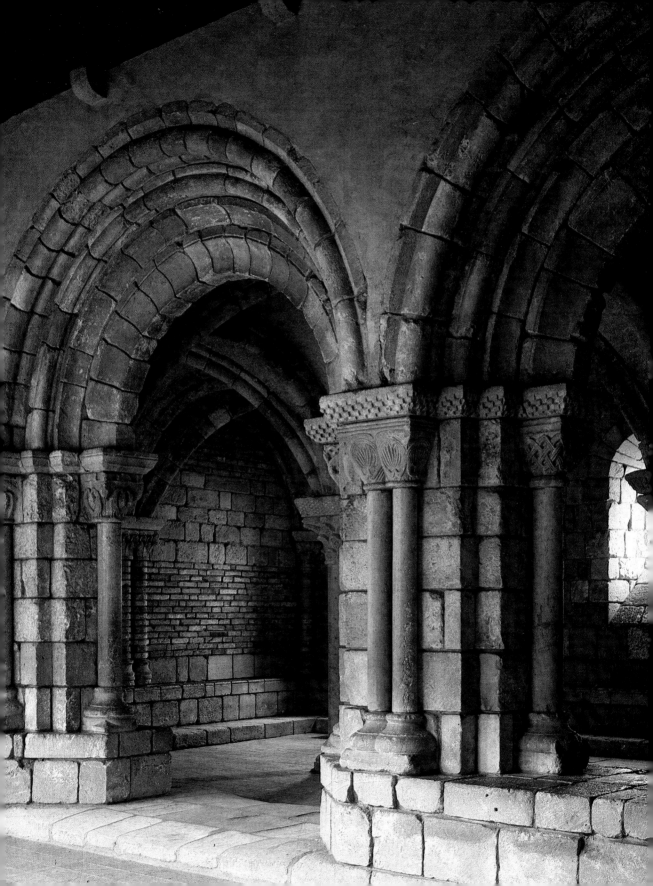

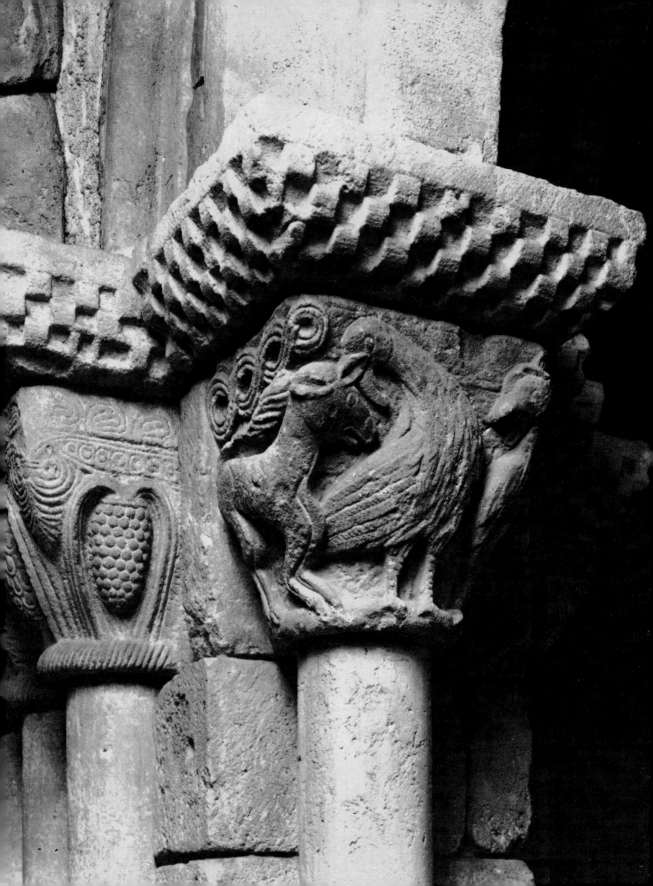

OPPOSITE PAGE:

*Animal and bird capital. Background: capital
with grape and pine cone motifs.*

*One of the center columns, its
capital carved with stars and
stylized leaf forms, its abacus with
rosettes.*

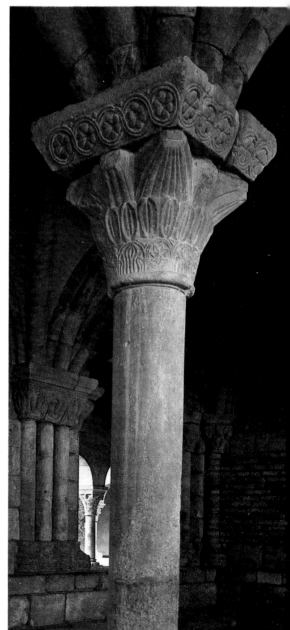

modern.) The exposed stones are of soft yellow limestone, which was quarried at some distance from the abbey and transported to the site. One wall shows several courses of brick, probably a substitute for stone depleted before the work was finished. The floor is not original but was modeled on twelfth-century tiles from the church at Cuxa.

The decorations of the capitals, abacus blocks, and keystone bosses of the vaults are imaginatively varied and include stars, rosettes, palmettes and other leaf forms, scrolls, basketweave patterns, and confronted birds picking at grapes or pine cones. The bird and pine cone composition may have been inspired by a Near Eastern brocade with a similar theme, for such textiles were greatly admired in the West in the medieval period. On nearly all of the capitals the decoration is purely ornamental, but on one, two giant birds, possibly a cock and a goose, seem to be intimidating a donkey-like animal—perhaps an illustration of an animal fable.

Over the centuries, like so many church buildings, the abbey of Pontaut suffered from changing political fortunes and neglect: it was partially destroyed in 1569 by the Huguenots, abandoned by 1791, and has now disappeared from all but the most detailed maps of the region.

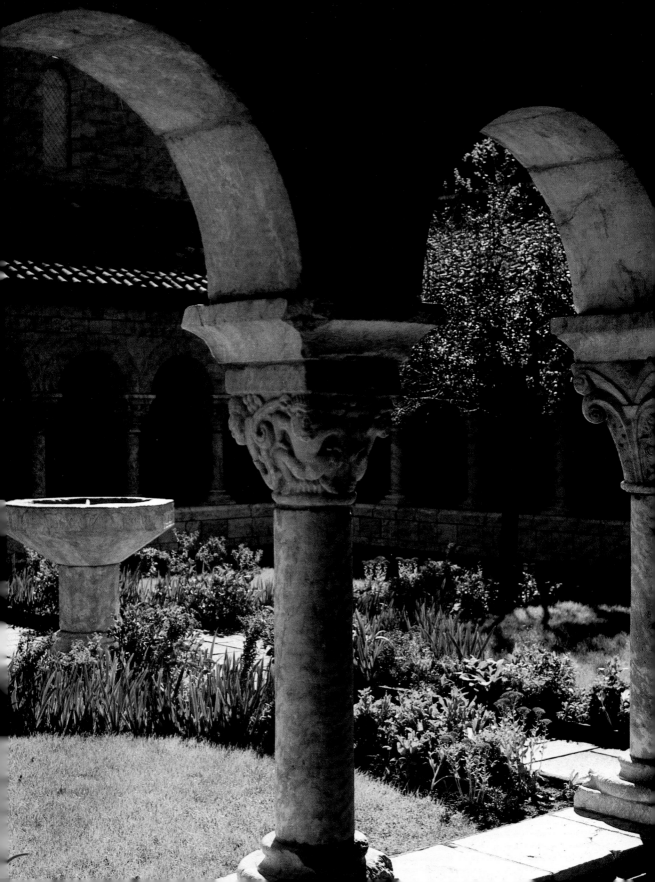

THE CUXA CLOISTER

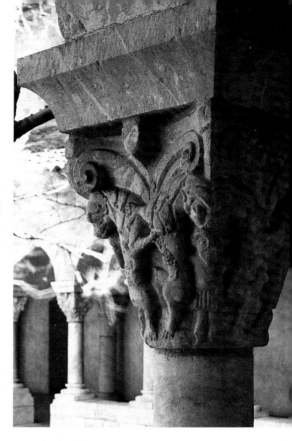

The Benedictine monastery of Saint-Michel-de-Cuxa, located at the foot of Mount Canigou in the northeast Pyrenees, was founded in 878. Its cloister, seen here in part, was built in the twelfth century. In 1654 the monastery was sacked by French troops in a period of hostilities between France and Spain. Long years of decline followed. In 1791, when France decreed the Civilian Constitution of the Clergy, the last of Cuxa's monks departed. The roof of the ancient church collapsed in 1835; the north bell tower fell in 1839. Subsequently, the monastery's stonework was dispersed. Until 1906 some of the columns were with those now in the Saint-Guilhem Cloister, in a private garden near Montpellier.

From a plan of the monastery dated 1779, some notes and drawings made by visitors early in the nineteenth century, and twentieth-century studies made at the site, it can be determined that the cloister once measured some 156 by 128 feet, or approximately twice what it measures here. The boldly cut marble capitals show great variety of design. Some are fashioned in the simplest of block forms, others are intricately carved with scrolling leaves, pine cones, animals with two bodies and a common head (a special breed for the corners of capitals), lions devouring people or else their own forelegs, lions restrained by apes, a leaping man blowing a horn, and a mermaid holding her tail. The mermaid capital, in the east arcade, differs in style and technique from the rest. The carving is more delicate, a drill was used for the details, and the creature's eyes are inlaid with lead.

OPPOSITE AND NEXT PAGES: *views of the Cuxa Cloister.*

South arcade: man wrestling with lions whose bodies unite in a single head.

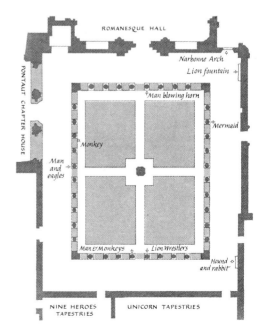

47

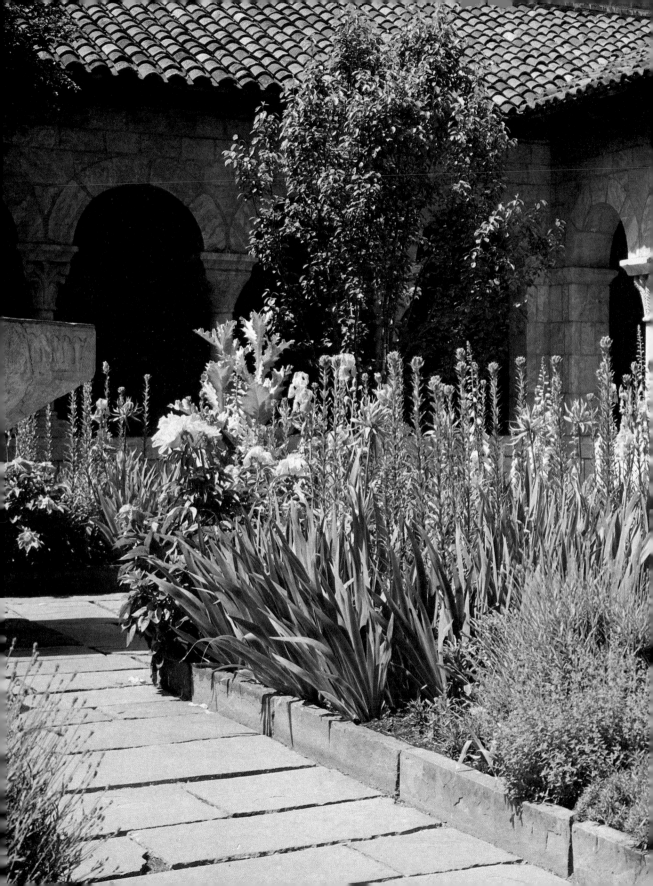

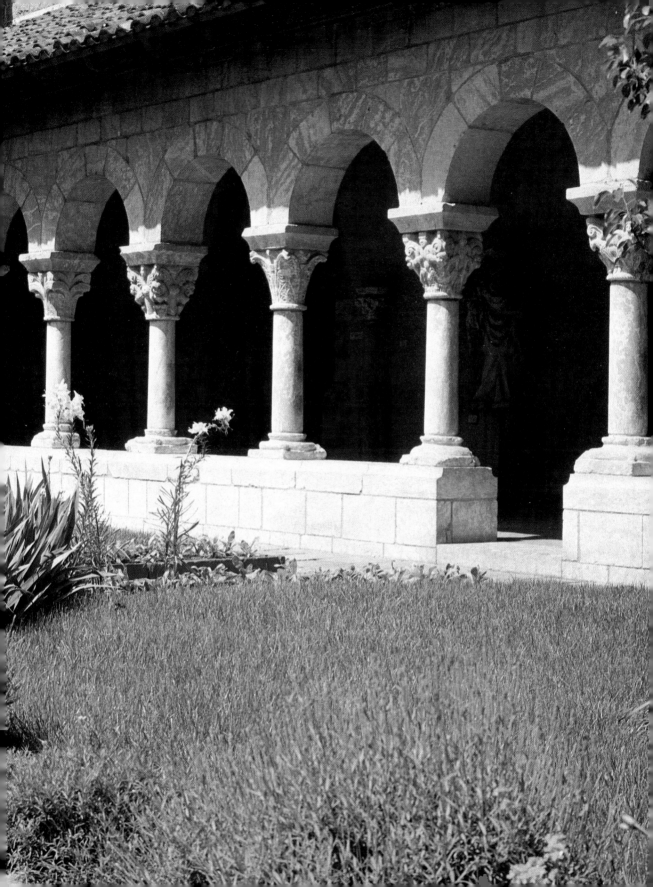

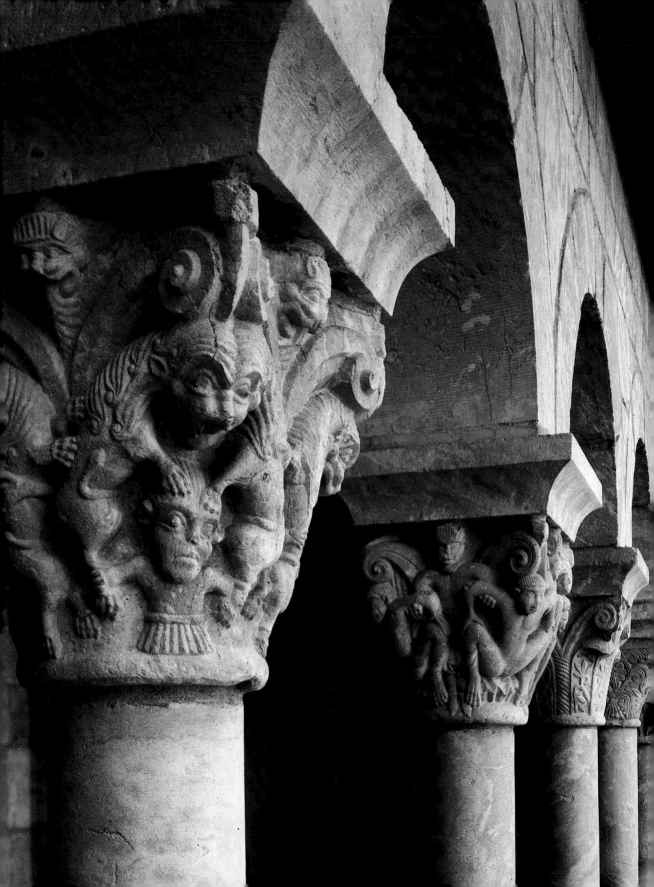

Some of the capitals, like one from Pontaut (p. 42) suggest influences from Near Eastern textile designs with animal compositions. Others, again like one in the Chapter House, appear to derive from fables or the imaginative lore preserved in bestiaries. Many of the motifs doubtless represent Christian versions of the struggle between the forces of good and evil, but for the Cuxa artists conveying the old meanings seemed to be less important than creating striking compositions.

Clearly embodying popular thought as recorded in the moralizing bestiaries is an arch said to have come from a twelfth-century church in Narbonne, not far from Cuxa.

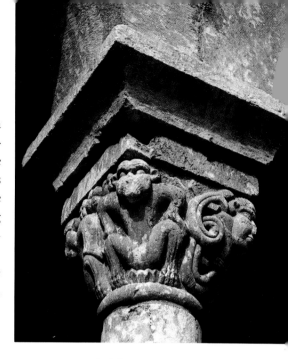

OPPOSITE PAGE: *south arcade: another view of lion-wrestlers and, next capital, a man grasping monkeys.*

BELOW: *west arcade: men with Oriental faces, grasping eagles; and east arcade: stylized palm tree with peering heads.*

ABOVE: *an ape with merman.*

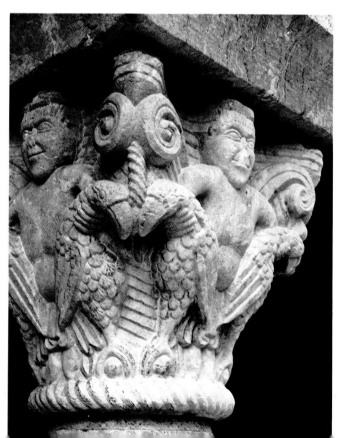

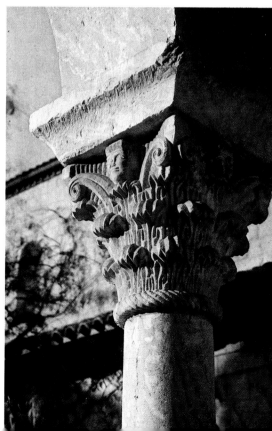

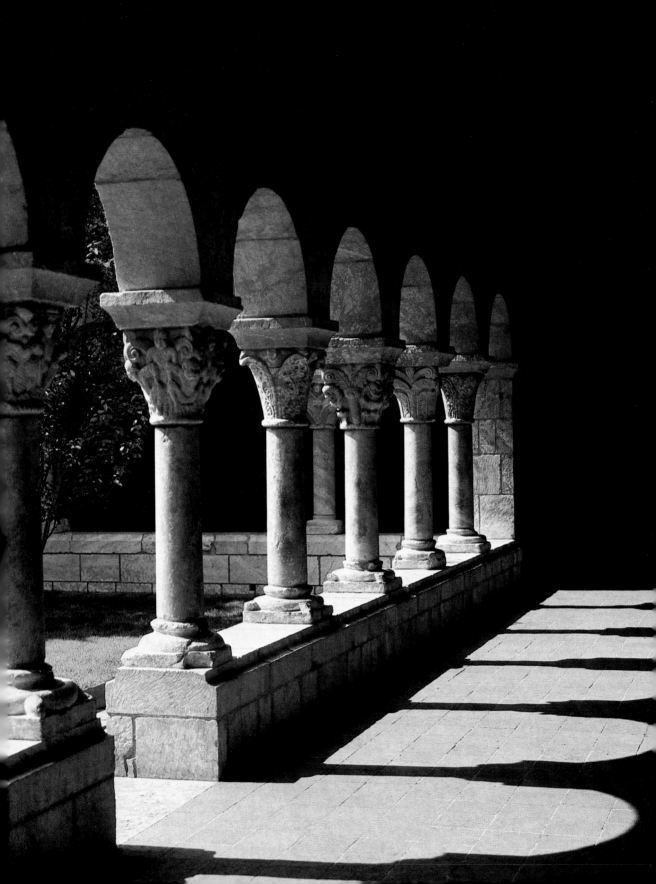

The arch surmounts the door in the cloister's northeast corner, leading the eye over the doorway with the undulating forms of a variety of fantastic beasts. Expansively filling their alloted spaces on the rounded marble blocks are a manticore, pelican, basilisk, harpy, griffin, amphisbaena (or possibly a dragon), centaur, and lion. All of

OPPOSITE PAGE:

west arcade, morning.

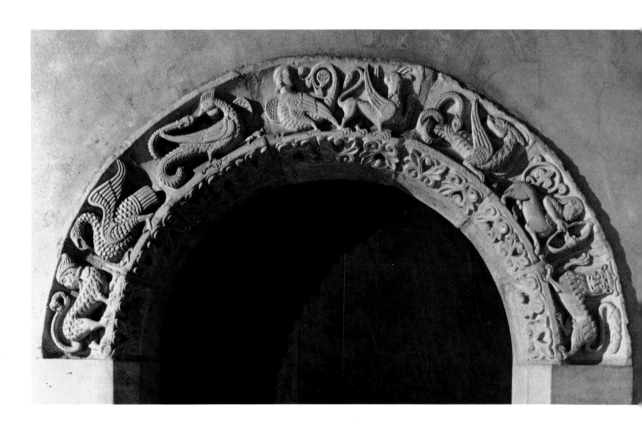

The Narbonne arch: the manticore (left end), with a man's face, lion's body, and scorpion's tail, has only its flutelike voice to recommend it. The harpy (at top), with her beautiful voice and false music, lures sailors to their doom. The griffin, with body and claws of the lion and wings and beak of the eagle, feasts on men. The two-headed amphisbaena, belonging to the reptile class like the dragon, can move equally well in either direction. The centaur, a forest creature of great intelligence, is ruled by animal passions.

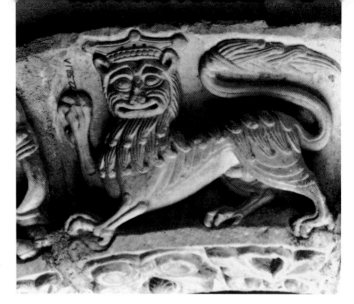

On the Narbonne arch: the lion, who erases his tracks with his tail when hunted, symbolizes Christ's incarnation.

So frightful that it can kill with a look or a hiss, the basilisk is itself killed by the weasel, signifying that God made nothing without a cure.

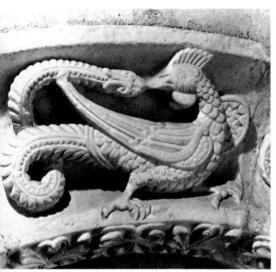

these creatures, whether completely imaginary or merely exotic, were tangibly real to many in the Middle Ages, and the dangers of the basilisk, harpy, and griffin were then as commonly feared as the inspirational virtues of the pelican and lion were admired.

Just to the right of the Narbonne arch is a fountain and basin made of the same mottled red and grayish white marble used for the Cuxa stonework, which was quarried not far from the monastery. The fountain, originally from the monastery of Notre-Dame-du-Vilar, a little east of Cuxa, issues a flow of water from the mouth of a lion's head, carved in the Cuxa style. The basin, simply carved in an interlace pattern, may have served as a reservoir for

The pelican pierces her breast so that her blood, falling upon her dead offspring, will bring them back to life—her sacrifice symbolizing that of Christ's.

OPPOSITE PAGE:
Fountain and basin from Notre-Dame-du-Vilar. 12th century.

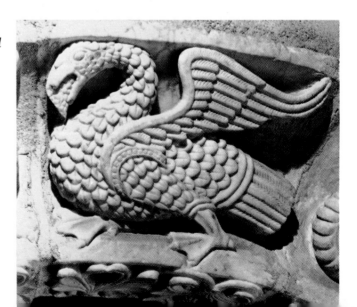

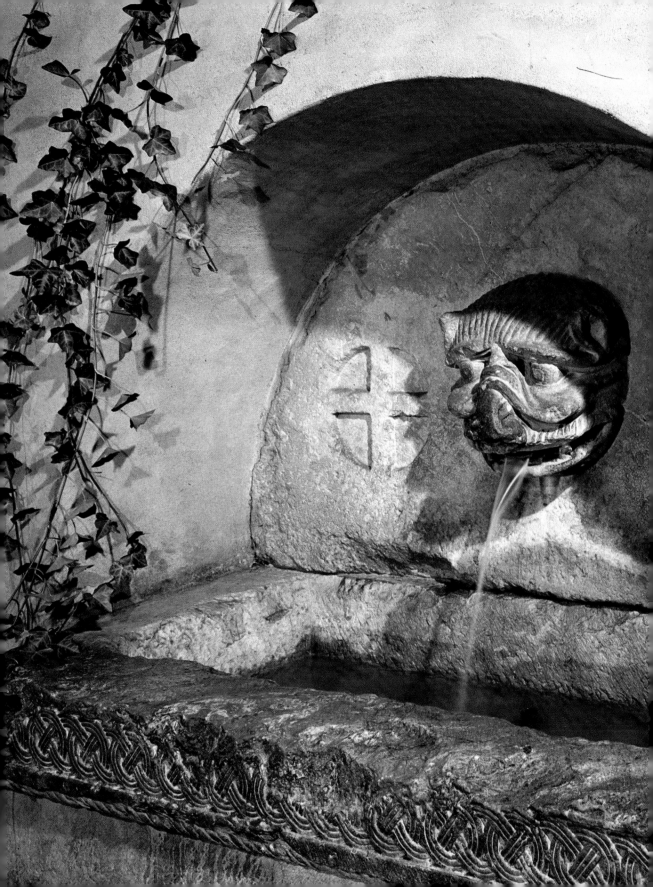

the filling of buckets or a lavabo for the washing of hands. In many monasteries, a lavabo was located near the refectory, either recessed into the wall of the cloister walk or housed in the courtyard in a small covered pavilion of its own.

The cloister garden is transversed by crosswalks, which—whether or not they performed the additional function of symbolism—provided rapid access from one part of the monastery to another. As in most monasteries, a source of water occupies the center of the cross—here, an eight-sided fountain from a neighboring monastery, Saint-Genis-des-Fontaines.

Like those in the Chapter House, the floor tiles of the arcades are modeled after ones excavated from the old walks at Cuxa, and the plaster walls, simple beamed and planked ceilings resting on corbels, and the tile roofs in the Mediterranean style all follow Cuxa precedents.

Many doors and windows from old French houses are to be found in The Cloisters. Beneath the sill of this 15th-century window in the wall of the east walk a hound confronts a rabbit.

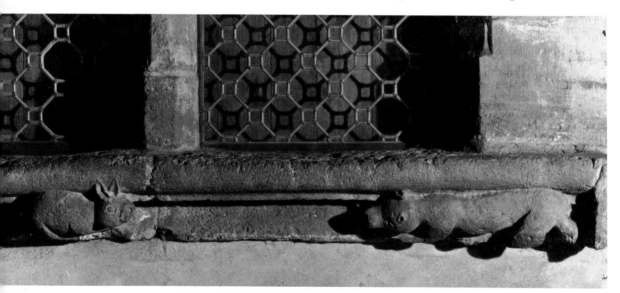

OPPOSITE PAGE: *the central fountain, from the monastery of Saint-Genis-des-Fontaines, not far from Cuxa, was possibly once a font.*

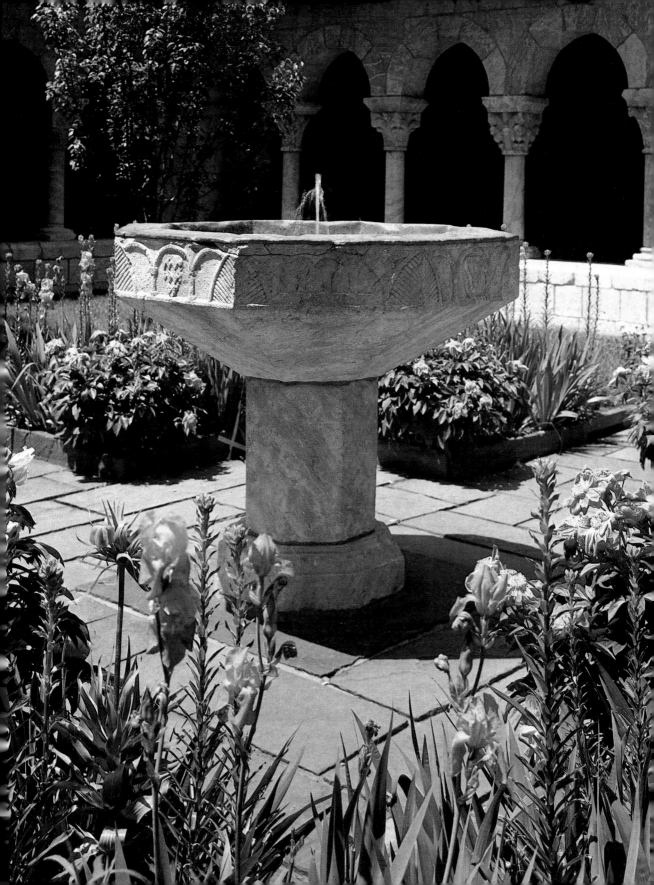

THE NINE HEROES
TAPESTRIES ROOM

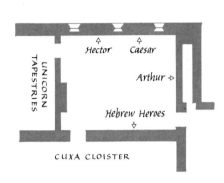

Limestone door, flamboyant Gothic style. French. 15th century.

From the Cuxa Cloister one enters this room through a door in the flamboyant Gothic style. In France, by the fifteenth century, the simple pointed Gothic arch was often elaborated in flamboyant, or "flamelike," designs of double curves, with a superstructure ornamented with stylized leaf forms, cusps, and pinnacles, all enhancing the arch's feeling of soaring upward movement and liveliness. This particular door is a modest example of its kind; others at The Cloisters are more elaborate in decoration and more exuberant in style.

Made around 1385, the Nine Heroes Tapestries are one of the two sets that survive from this early period. Because the other set—the Apocalypse tapestries at Angers, in France—closely resembles this one in design, choice of colors, and fabric construction, the Nine Heroes have been attributed to the same source in Paris: the workshop of Nicolas Bataille. Originally, there were three hangings, each more than twenty-one feet wide, each containing the likenesses of three heroic figures. Not unexpectedly, they show damages and losses, but even in their fragmented state, they offer remarkable glimpses into medieval court life.

The chivalrous theme of the Heroes was popularized in about 1310 by the jongleur Jacques de Longuyon. Porus, the protagonist, was represented in the poem as a hero who fought more bravely than the nine great heroes of old. As selected by Longuyon, these nine comprised three pagan heroes: Hector, Alexander, and Julius Caesar; three Hebrew: David, Joshua, and Judas Maccabeus; and three Christian: Arthur, Charlemagne, and Godfrey

58

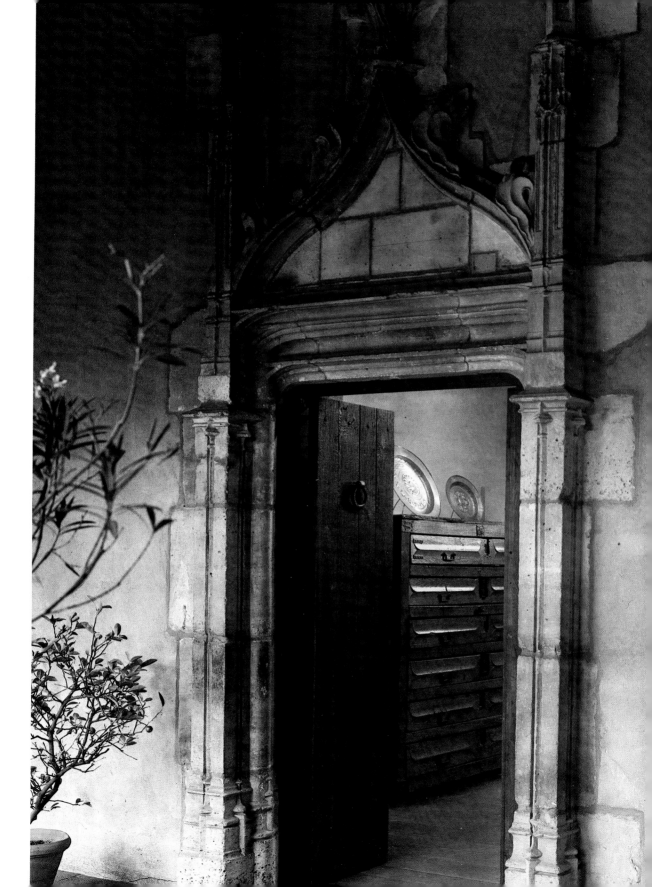

The table and the seat, both of the 15th century, are carved with linen-fold panels. The tapestry figure at the left is Hector, one of the pagan heroes.

of Bouillon. The symbolism of this company, of three and three times three, inspired works in all of the arts: the Nine Heroes were soon interpreted in sculpture, frescoes, manuscript illuminations, and even playing cards.

It was a typical penchant of medieval artists to portray the ancients in contemporary dress, and Nicolas Bataille's heroes, no matter what their era, are sumptuously clad and accoutered in the style of around 1380. King David, in crown and ermine and with a golden harp, poses im-

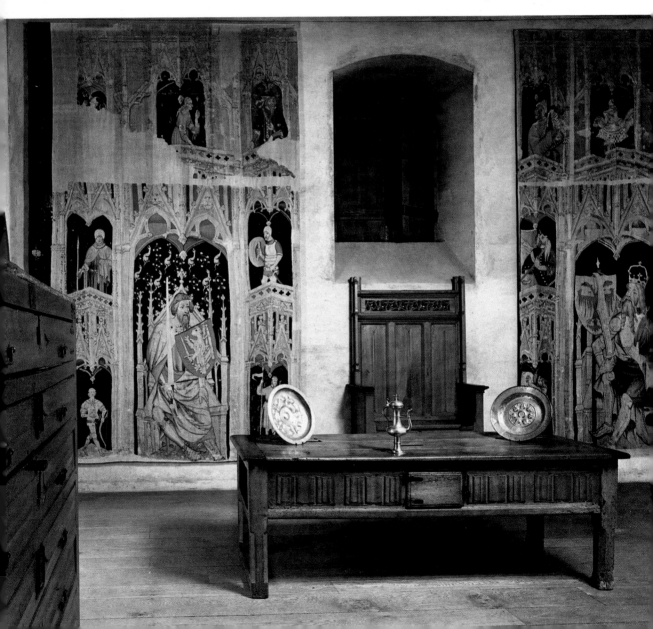

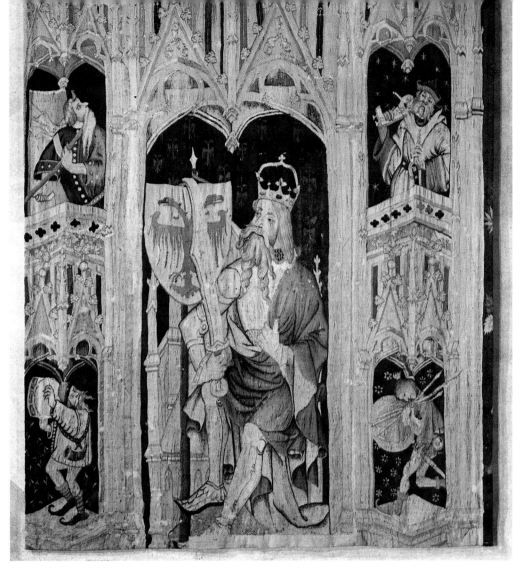

perially in a vaulted niche at the center of the Hebrews tapestry. At his left is Joshua, a winged dragon on his shield and the "sun in its glory" on the cloth beneath his armored feet. In the tapestry with the pagan worthies, which is better preserved than the other two, Hector has a shield with a lion seated in a chair and Caesar is identified by his customary medieval coat of arms of double-headed eagle in sable on gold. Arthur, with the golden crowns of England, Scotland, and Brittany on his surcoat and banner, is the only Christian hero to remain.

Julius Caesar, identified by his blazon of double-headed eagle, is surrounded by court entertainers.

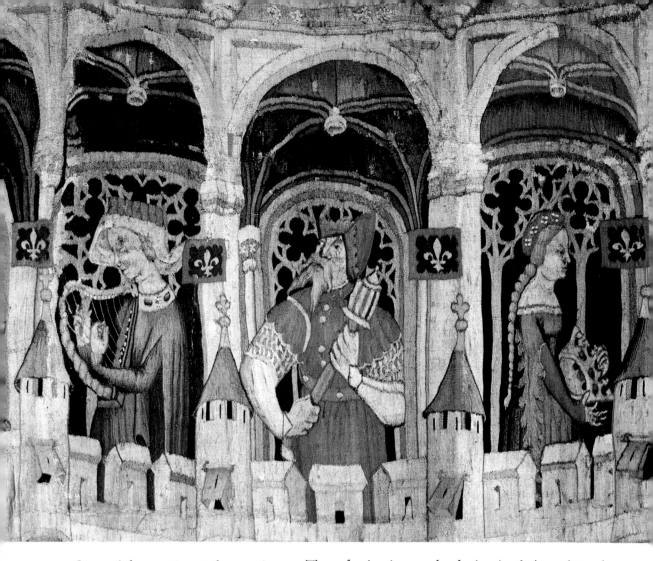

Some of the courtiers at the top of the Hebrews tapestry. The arms seen on most of the banners (and elsewhere in this tapestry) are those of Jean, duke of Berry (1340–1416).

These fascinating works depict, in their variety, the highest level of a rich and powerful social structure of late fourteenth-century France. The little figures in the surrounding arcades, doubtless no more than types, represent the members of a medieval court: bishops, cardinals, knights, ladies, musicians, spearmen, and archers. The churchmen appear with the Christian hero; the more frivolous figures are grouped around the pagan and Hebrew heroes.

Such elaborate works of fine craftsmanship were no doubt made for a noble patron, and the tapestries them-

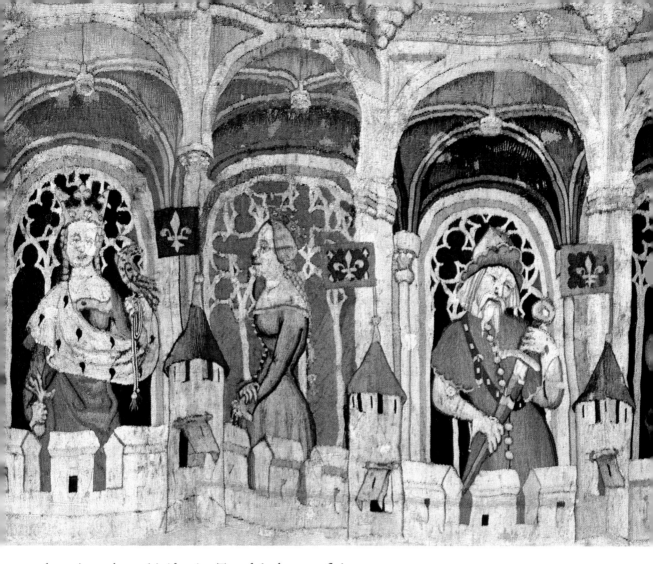

selves give a clue to his identity. Ten of the banners flying from the turrets of the Hebrews tapestry, as well as escutcheons in the vaults above David and Joshua, display the arms of Jean, duke of Berry: the fleur-de-lis of France on azure with indented red border. Jean, the younger brother of Charles V of France, was one of the greatest art patrons of the Middle Ages, and the prominence of his arms in this set indicates that the tapestries were commissioned either by him or for him. Most of the Angers Apocalypse tapestries, so close to these in style and technique, were made for Jean's brother, Louis, duke of Anjou.

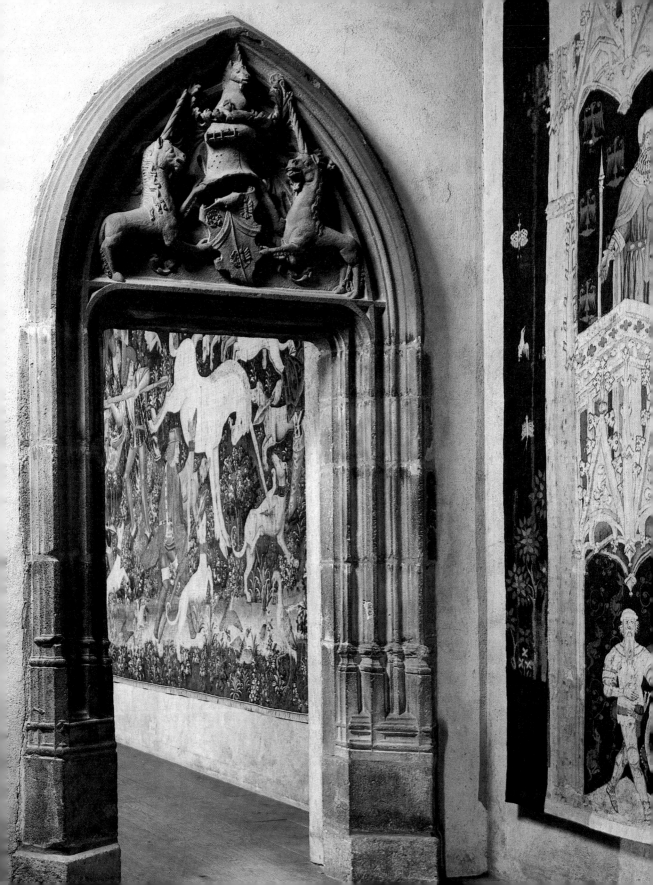

THE UNICORN
TAPESTRIES ROOM

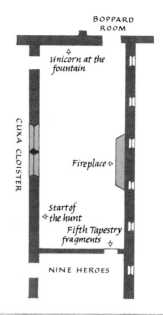

In this room, which one may enter from the Nine Heroes Room through an early sixteenth-century door carved with unicorns supporting a shield, is one of The Cloisters' most admired possessions: the set of tapestries called the Hunt of the Unicorn.

A great deal has been learned about these magnificent hangings in modern times: where they must have been woven—Brussels, in view of their technique and style—and approximately when, for particulars of the men's and women's costumes establish the time of the design around 1500. Furthermore, close correspondences have been discovered between several of the men and women in the tapestries and figures in Parisian prints and miniature paintings of the period, showing that the designer was familiar with French art.

But beyond these matters of technique and style and comparison, there is a mystery. The commissioner of the weavings is no longer known, nor is the occasion for which this extraordinary set was produced.

Much investigative work has been done on the tied AE's that are so prominent in all the designs, and on the equally tantalizing FR that has long been associated with the third tapestry even though it is not part of the basic

OPPOSITE PAGE: *early 16th-century door of volcanic stone. Montferrand, Auvergne.*

Sixth tapestry: courtiers watching the unicorn hunt from the castle.

65

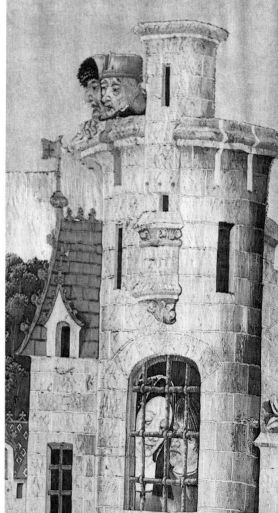

The furnishings
in this likeness
of a nobleman's
hall include a
covered beaker
(German, Frank-
fort; mid-17th
century), made of
narwhal tusk,
regarded for cen-
turies as the horn
of the unicorn.
Installed in the
late Gothic win-
dow are panels
of stained glass
(Flemish; early
16th century)
containing the
arms of Emperor
Maximilian I,
his son Philip
the Fair, his
grandson Prince
Charles, and one
of his councilors.

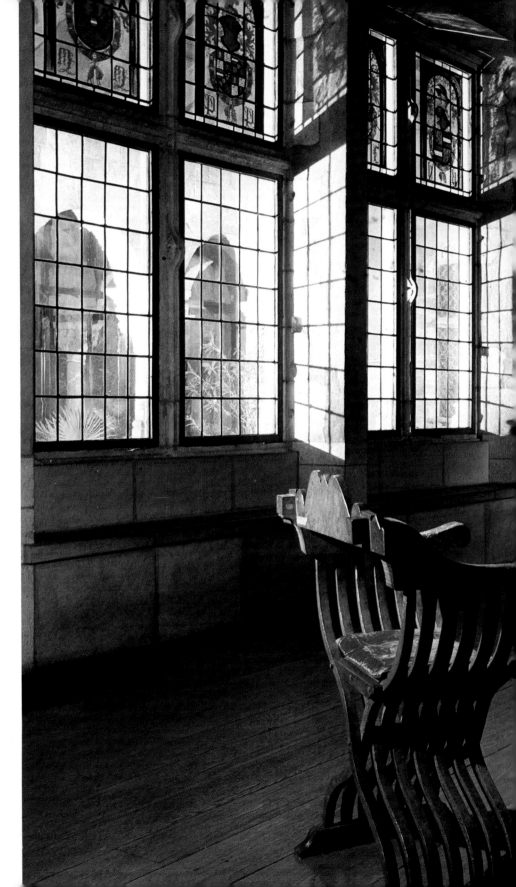

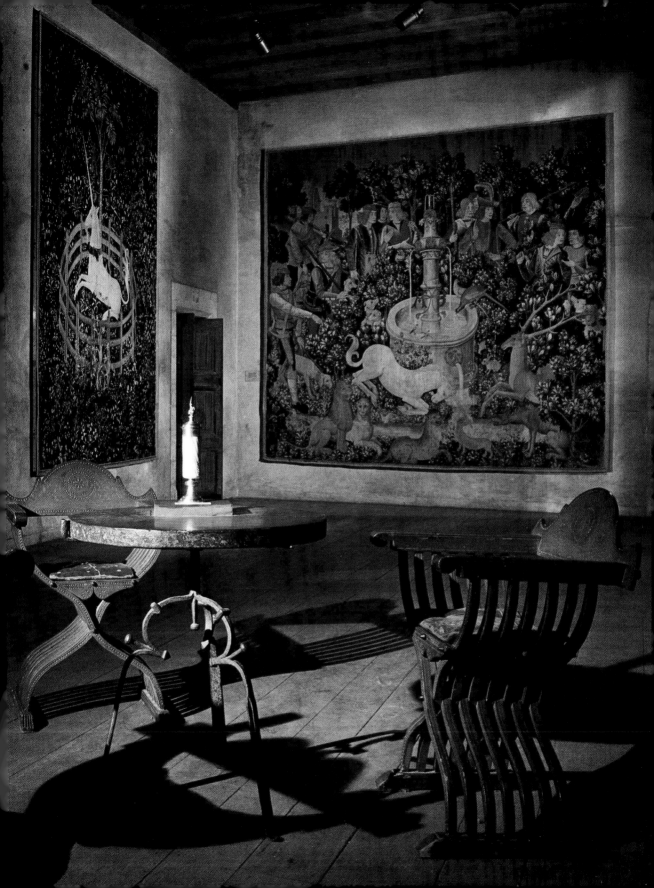

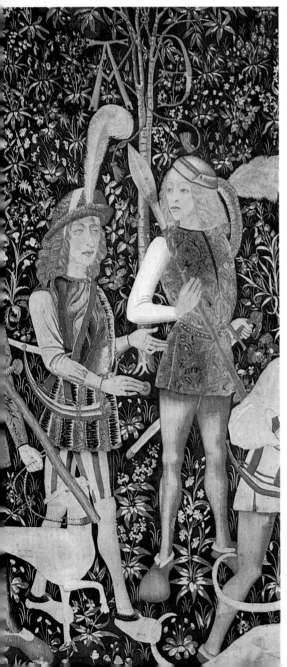

First tapestry: the enigmatic AE is placed at the center and repeated in the corners.

fabric. And the other seeming clues have been repeatedly studied: the coat of arms on the collar of a dog in the first tapestry, inscriptions on the collars of dogs in the fourth and fifth tapestries, inscriptions on hunters' horns in the second and third. Though many theories have been proposed, none has been conclusively proved. Meanwhile, the old records that would identify both the commissioner and the recipient of the set—assuming that it was commissioned as a gift—have been searched for in vain.

The oldest document that mentions the tapestries is an inventory made March 18, 1680, of the possessions of François VI de la Rochefoucauld, the author of the once much read Maxims. The seven tapestries, this document reveals, were that day hanging in the duke's bed chamber in Paris. (The present setting for the tapestries evokes a castle hall, with its massive fireplace and its large window from a late Gothic house in Cluny.) After 1680 the tapestries continued in the possession of the La Rochefoucauld family. In 1793, during the Revolution, they were taken from the family's château at Verteuil, south of Paris, and for a generation or so used to protect peasants' fruit trees and vegetables from freezing. The heaviest of the damages doubtless occurred during this period, including the loss of most of the fifth tapestry and important parts of the others. (The present skies are modern. The original sky areas may have been filled with bands of inscriptions, for large blank spaces in tapestries were not to the medieval taste.) In the 1850s, interested in recovering some of his family's possessions, Count Hippolyte de La Rochefoucauld learned of some "old curtains" lying in a barn. Soon afterward the tapestries once again hung in the château.

In no other work of art, large or small, is the symbolic pursuit and killing of the unicorn presented in such astonishing detail. Even the botanically accurate trees and flowering plants have roles to play in the story.

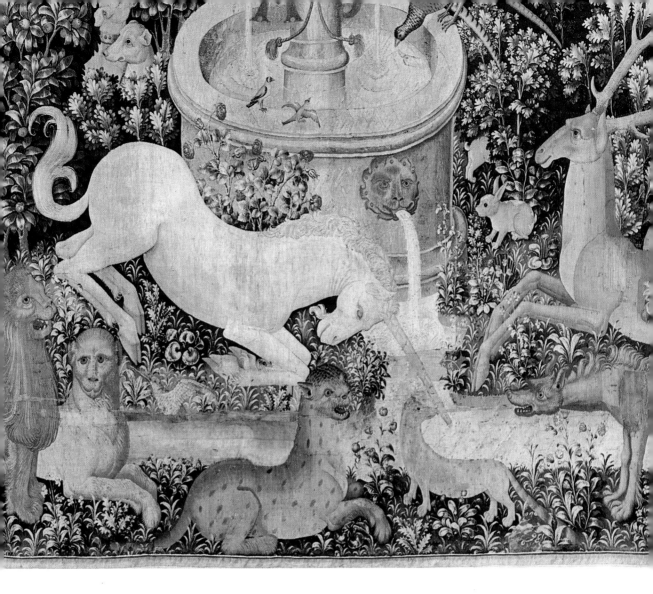

In the first tapestry, against a flat background of violets, daisies, strawberries, and periwinkles, the lord of the hunt and his companions set forth on their quest. On leash are greyhounds, which chase by sight, and running hounds, which chase by scent. One of the party calls in the distance that the quarry has been sighted. Thus far it is possible to believe that the quarry will be the fleet stag of so many medieval hunts depicted in art, but in the second tapestry the hunters gather at a fountain in a naturalistic

Second tapestry: the unicorn purifies the water.

69

Third tapestry: a running hound.

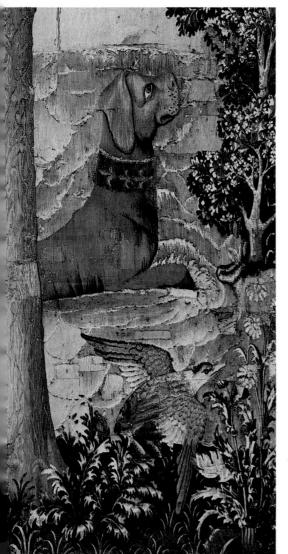

forest to watch a milk-white unicorn dip his purifying horn into a stream that has been poisoned by the serpent—that is, by the Devil. Waiting to drink the water in safety are creatures whose natures were praised by writers of medieval lore. The panther, good-tempered, gentle, intelligent, and wondrously sweet-smelling, was loved by all animals except the dragon and was considered by men to be a symbol of Christ. The noble and valiant lion, sleeping ever with his eyes open, resurrected his cubs, born dead, by roaring over them on the third day. The stag, a destroyer of dangerous serpents, set lessons for Christians in the ways he protected his kind against the hazards of life. Even the hyena, acknowledged to be a mirror of the wickedness in man, had his virtues, notably in a spleen that could be used to restore clearness of eyesight and in a gem, residing in his eye, that would enable its possessor to foretell the future.

In the third and fourth tapestries the hunt is on in earnest, with the unicorn demonstrating what seemingly everyone but huntsmen always knew: that he could never be taken by ordinary methods. Confirming his supernatural role, the hunter who blows his horn in the fourth tapestry represents God's messenger, the angel Gabriel;

70

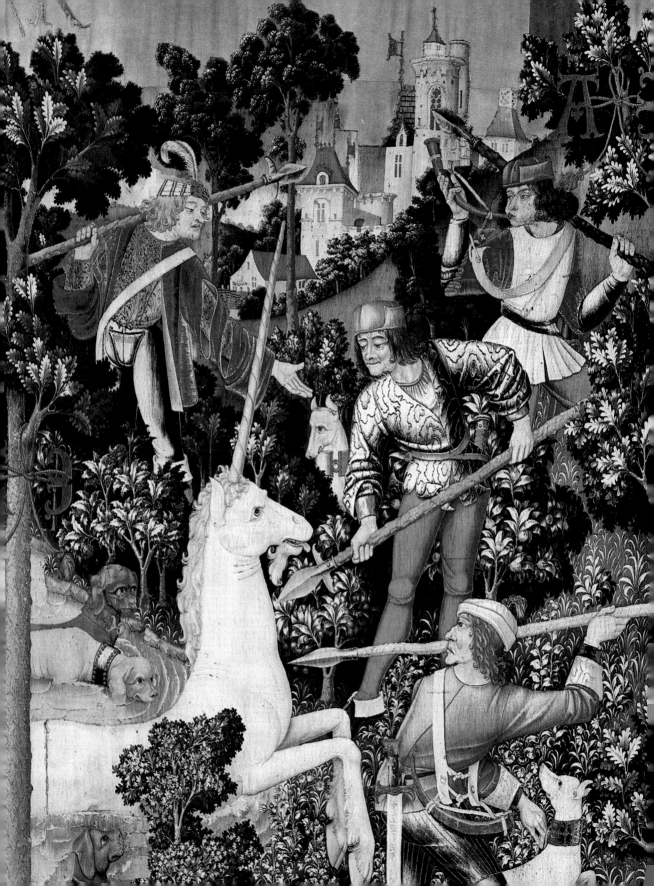

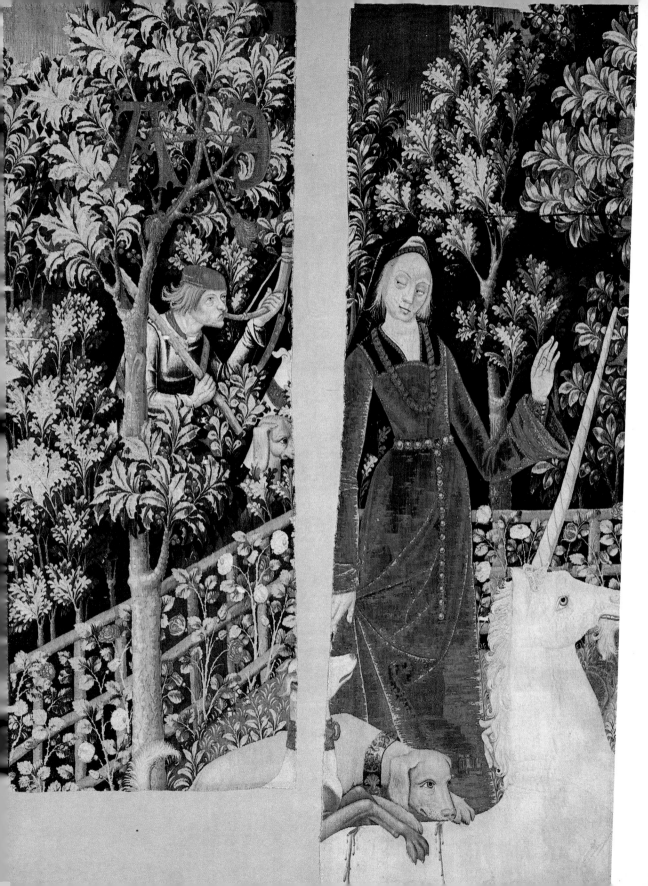

the words "Ave Regina C" (Hail, Queen of Heaven) are inscribed upon his scabbard.

In what remains of the fifth tapestry the unicorn comes eagerly to the lap of a maid whose arm and fingers encircle his neck. Medieval authorities agreed on the essentials of this episode: As the unicorn surrendered his fierceness and became tame and vulnerable through his encounter with a maid, so Christ apparently surrendered his divine nature and became a human being through the Virgin, for the salvation of mankind. The garden in which the unicorn and maiden meet, attended by a woman who seems to signal the hunters to wait, is the fenced garden of the Song of Songs: "A garden enclosed is my sister, my spouse." The roses blooming in the fence are symbolic of Mary, the white ones of her virginity, the red ones of her charity.

In the sixth tapestry, after his surrender in the fifth, the unicorn is slain and brought to the lord and lady of the castle, who are to benefit by possession of his magical horn. The horn of the dead animal is garlanded with oak branches that have unexpectedly produced thorns—and close by a hawthorn grows: the tree from which, the Middle Ages believed, Christ's crown was made. Above, where the unicorn is killed, a holly tree, known as Christ's thorn, denotes the Passion.

In the seventh tapestry, alive again and portrayed on another *millefleurs* ground, the unicorn is both the risen Christ and the lover-bridegroom acquiescently chained by his adored lady. The mingled imagery suggests that the tapestries were designed to celebrate a marriage, and many of the details reinforce the impression. What appears to be blood on the unicorn's body is juice dripping from the pomegranates in the tree above. Besides symbolizing the Church, Christ, and the promise of immortality, the pomegranate was a symbol of human fertility. The

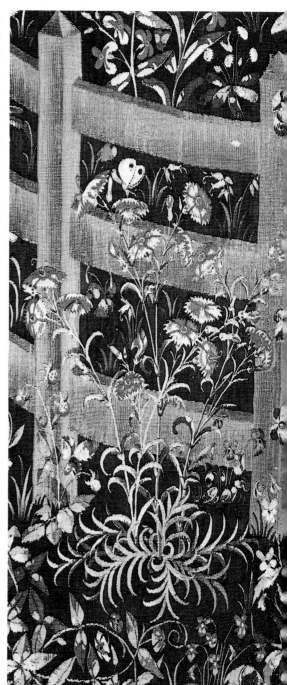

73

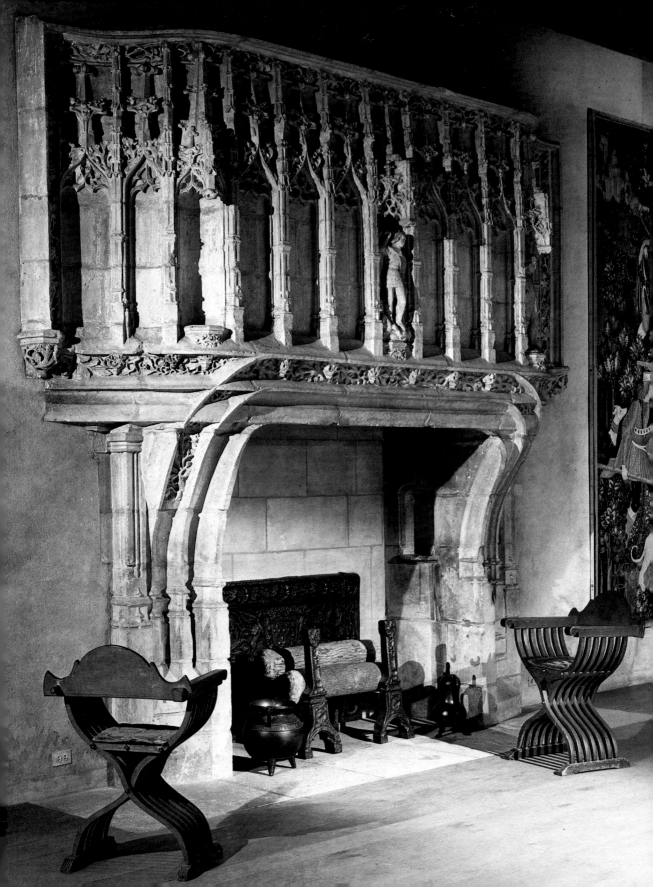

wild orchid, displayed so prominently against the unicorn's white body, was believed to be an aphrodisiac for both men and women. The bistort, flowering at his right foreleg, aided women to conceive. The carnation, growing against the fence, was associated with Christ and the Virgin and was also a flower of betrothal and marriage. The Madonna lily, in the right foreground, held by medieval authorities to be the lily of the Song of Songs, was a symbol of the purity of the Virgin, as well as a flower of faithfulness in love and marriage. Finally, the small green frog, seen just to the right of the Madonna lily, was reputed to have an aphrodisiac bone in its left side.

To explain the differences in the tapestries' backgrounds, it has been suggested that the central five, with their naturalistic settings, were designed to hang on walls, while the two with millefleurs grounds were made for the back and top of a canopied bed.

Modern viewers of this glorious set often speculate about the labor involved in covering the tough woolen warps with the plant-dyed weft, most of which is of wool, with some use of silk and metallic threads. The weavers produced the fabric from full-scale painted designs, or cartoons, forcing the weft threads tightly into place, each different-colored thread separately, until the entire undyed warp was concealed. Even with several weavers working side by side, the usual procedure, and with the tapestries at work simultaneously on separate looms, the commission would have taken several years.

Another point of interest is the source of the colors. Three plants only, it is known from analysis, made them all: madder the reds, weld the yellows, and woad the blues, with combinations of the dyes and changes in the mordants producing the seemingly endless range of subsidiary colors. All three of these dye plants, incidentally, are grown in the garden of the Bonnefont Cloister, along with many of the plants that appear in the tapestries.

75

OPPOSITE PAGE: *limestone fireplace. From Alençon, France. Flamboyant Gothic style, late 15th century.*

Seventh tapestry: the unicorn in captivity.

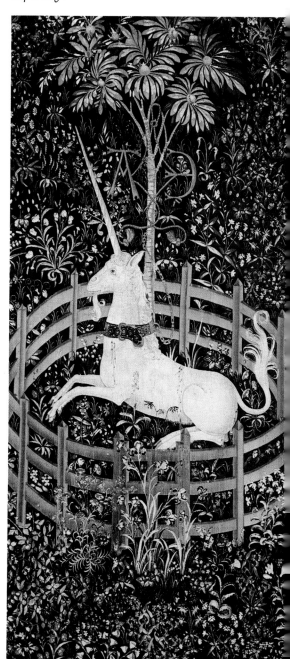

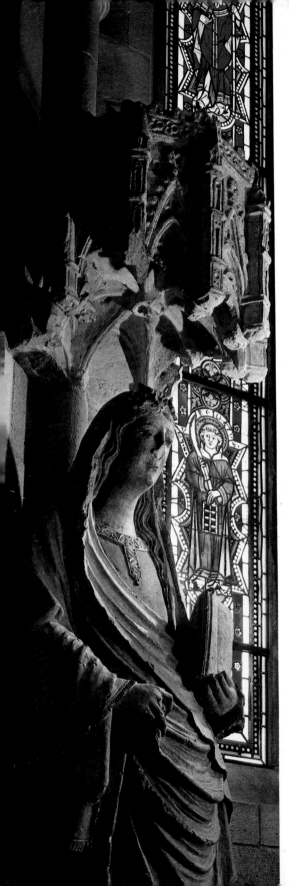

THE GOTHIC CHAPEL

Intended primarily as a setting for stained glass and large sculptures, this modern structure—rising two stories at The Cloisters' southwest corner—is in the Gothic style, with features suggested by thirteenth-century chapels at Carcasonne and Monsempron. An unglazed window with Gothic tracery at the top of the stairs provides a view down to the sculptures, and an imposing abbey door in the chapel's east wall leads out to the Glass Gallery and the Bonnefont Cloister.

The pointed Gothic arch is the element that made the high bayed ceiling of such structures possible, and ribbed vaults, supported by buttresses on the exterior, permitted the thick walls and small windows of the Romanesque

In the apse: sculpture of Saint Margaret. Said to come from the old cathedral of Lérida, Spain. About 1330. Limestone with polychromy.

OPPOSITE PAGE: *the Gothic Chapel seen from the Early Gothic Hall.*

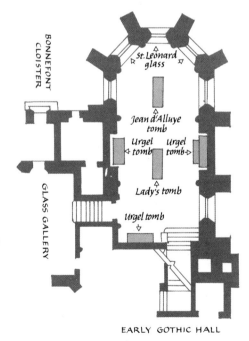

BONNEFONT CLOISTER

St. Leonard glass

Jean d'Alluye tomb

Urgel tomb   Urgel tomb

GLASS GALLERY

Lady's tomb

Urgel tomb

EARLY GOTHIC HALL

76

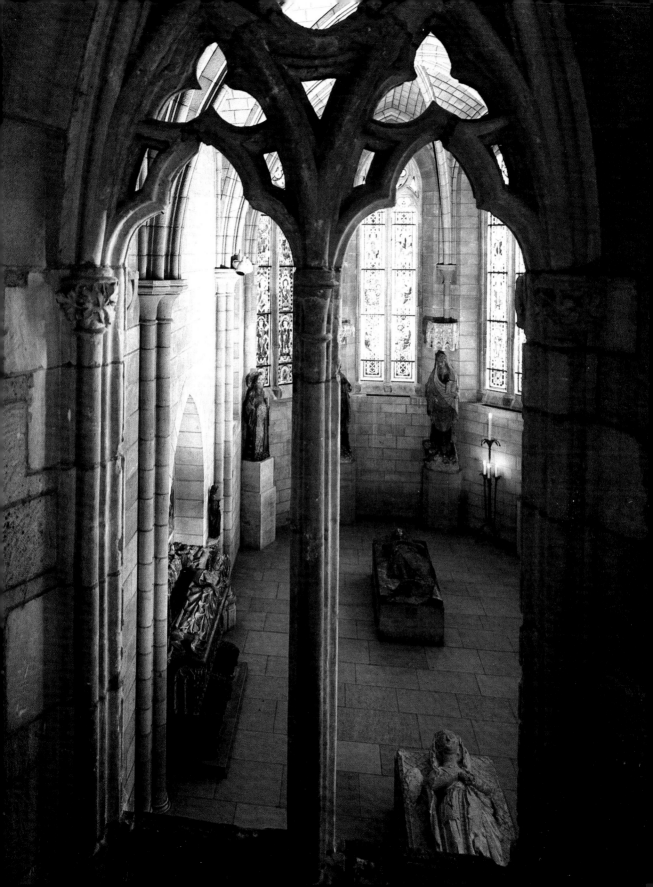

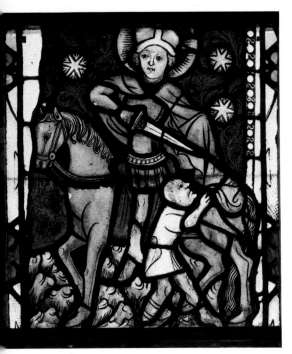

Stained-glass panel with Saint Martin dividing his cloak with the beggar. Austrian. Second half of 14th century.

OPPOSITE PAGE: *stained-glass panels with Isaiah and Mary Magdalen. Possibly from the abbey of Evron, Normandy. About 1325.*

period to be exchanged for the Gothic "cage of stone," whose wide and lofty openings were ideal spaces for shimmering, glowing compositions of glass.

Though the coloring of glass was practiced in ancient times, the oldest colored glass windows were made in the eleventh century. The Gothic stained-glass window, the glazier's ultimate achievement, was a triumph of the twelfth and thirteenth centuries.

To make his composition, the artist first drew his design on vellum, perhaps at quarter scale, then enlarged it to size on a whitened board. His glass, colored by the addition to the melt of metal oxides (cobalt, copper, iron, manganese), was placed on the board and the underlying shape traced on its surface. Controlled breaking was effected by brushing the trace line with water and passing a heated iron along it. Next, the coloring that provided form and feature was painted on and fired to permanence in a kiln. The finished pieces were then surrounded with lead cames, double-channeled to accept the adjoining pieces. After assembly, the cames were soldered together and one or more iron bars were attached to the panel for strength. The completed panels were fastened into the window by attachment to frames already fixed in the stone.

Although there are examples of twelfth- and thirteenth-century glass elsewhere in The Cloisters, all the glass in the Gothic Chapel is of the fourteenth century.

The three center windows of the five in the apse contain glass from the church of Saint Leonhard in Lavanttal, southern Austria, built around 1340. The childlike simplicity of the figural scenes contrasts with the richly ornamented areas that frame and separate them. Complicated medallion frames were seen in stained-glass windows throughout the German empire in this period. The panels in the first and fifth of the apse windows are also Austrian, but of a later period, around 1390, and are much more elegant in style. The Annunciation panel in the

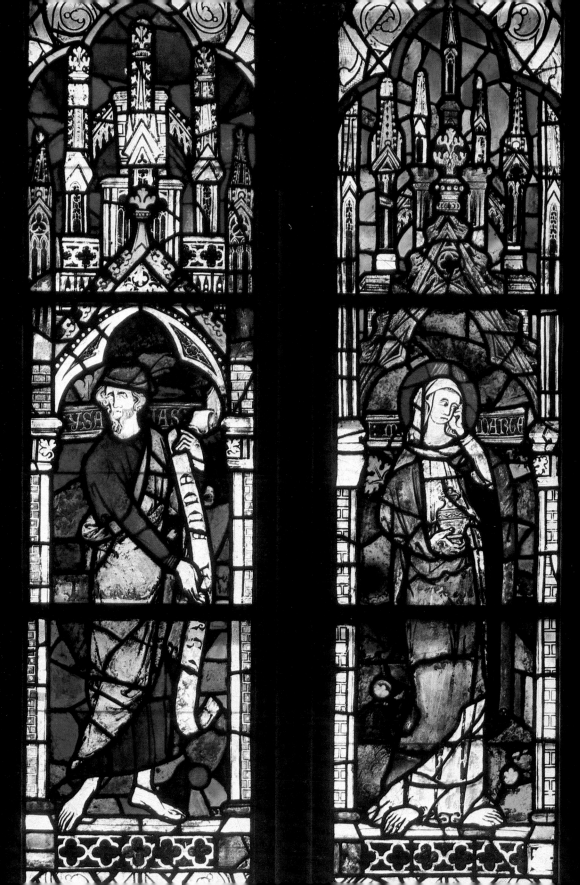

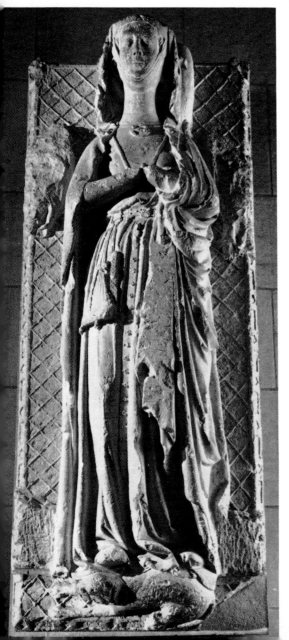

OPPOSITE PAGE: *the chapel from the apse, showing abbey door to the left (French; flamboyant style, late 15th or early 16th century).*

Effigy of a lady (Margaret of Gloucester?). French. Late 13th century.

leftmost window, which came from the castle chapel at Ebreichsdorf, reflects the court style of Vienna.

The glass in the west wall, just at the foot of the stairs, is thought to have come from the abbey of Evron, in Normandy, which was completed about 1325. The figures of Isaiah and Mary Magdalen, standing beneath soaring canopies made of white glass, are attenuated to fill the typical tall, narrow spaces of fourteenth-century church windows. Isaiah holds a scroll prophesying the birth of the Son. The grieving Mary Magdalen, her bare feet denoting the penitent sinner, suggests the passage in the Gospel of Saint John in which she says, "They have taken away my Lord, and I know not where they have laid him." The colors of these panels are more somber than the brilliantly colored Saint Leonhard panels, and the pieces of glass are larger and fewer. The silvery grisaille glass seen at the bottom and top was often used to save part of the great cost of glazing entire windows in color. And in northern France, where the light was not so bright as in the south, windows of the more transparent grisaille were sometimes preferred. (The grisaille that completes the first and fifth windows in the apse is modern.)

IN WESTERN EUROPE in the late eleventh century persons of importance began to be commemorated with tombstones bearing their effigies. These sometimes were made into splendid monuments, as seen here in the tombs of the counts of Urgel, or they might be simple, inexpensive tomb slabs. But whatever the degree of personal importance, and however much or little was spent on the design and carving of these early effigies, they were not meant to be portraits but simply commemorations.

Sometimes a tomb sculpture was fashioned according to the instructions of the tomb's future occupant; on other occasions it might be commissioned for the remains of an ancestor dead for generations. Such sculpture acquired its

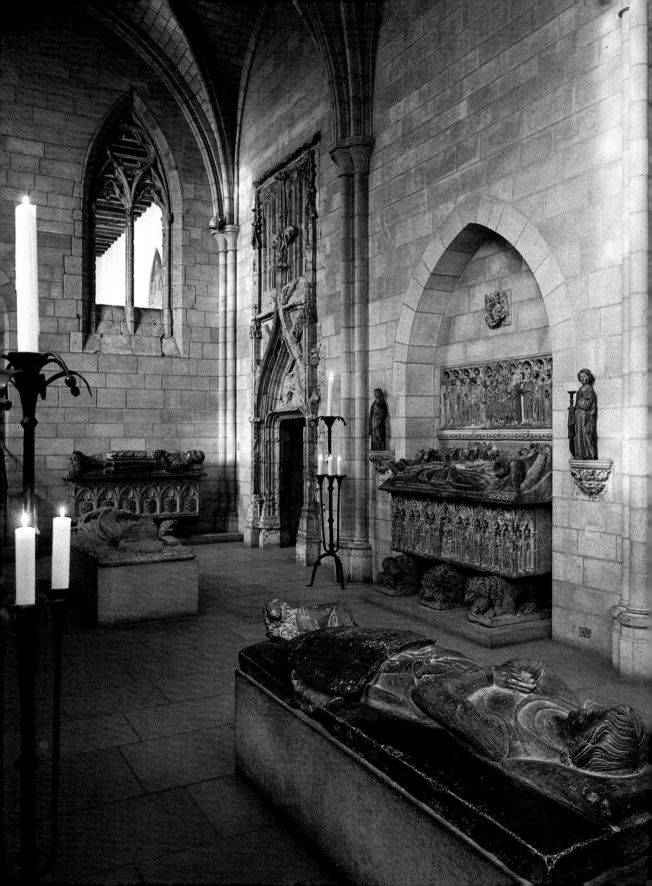

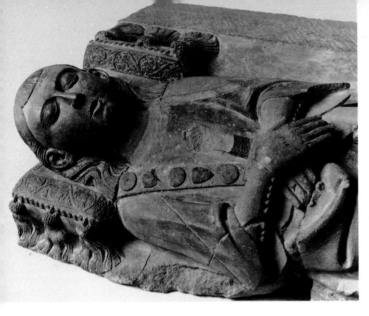

*Tomb effigy of a boy of the family
of the counts of Urgel. Spanish,
Léridan school. First half of 14th
century. The family arms are on
his shoulder strap.*

own conventions. A widespread one was a footrest for the recumbent figure, at a knight's feet usually a lion, testifying to his noble courage. At a woman's feet one often finds a small dog, symbolic of her fidelity and domesticity. Another convention was a sculptured group of mourners.

Of the four tombs in the Gothic Chapel once belonging to members of the Urgel family of Catalonia, the three largest have long been associated with the monastery of Bellpuig de las Avellanes, near Lérida in northeastern Spain. The small tomb effigy of a boy was in the nearby church of Santa Maria at Castelló de Farfanyá at least since the early nineteenth century. Although these tombs are among the finest surviving examples of sepulchral art of the Léridan school, dating from the first half of the fourteenth century, the tomb figures have never been positively identified.

It has been thought that the rebuilding of the church of Bellpuig de las Avellanes in the Catalonian Gothic style was undertaken by Ermengol X, who died in 1314, and that he intended to establish at this monastic church, long

82

under the patronage of the counts of Urgel, a family necropolis. The large tombs may therefore have been made in the same period, for Ermengol X and members of his immediate family. In his will, Ermengol X ordered that a fine tomb be made for himself and placed in the monastic church, and the earliest surviving descriptions of Las Avellanes identify the tomb with the effigy in chain mail and armor at the bottom of the steps as his. The double tomb is from the same workshop, and documentary evidence as well as the coats of arms suggest that these tombs were

Detail of sepulchral monument said to be that of Ermengol VII (died 1184). Assembled in 18th century. Effigy, first half of 14th century. Sarcophagus and celebrants relief, mid-14th century.

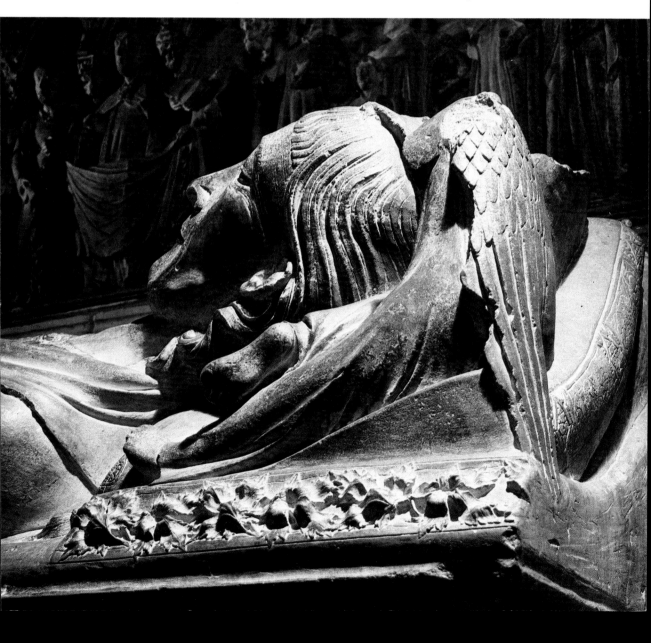

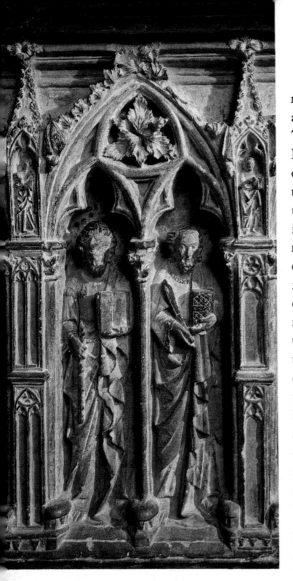

Detail of sarcophagus of Ermengol VII: two apostles.

OPPOSITE PAGE: *double tomb of members of the family of the counts of Urgel, possibly Alvaro Rodrigo de Cabrera, count of Urgel (died 1268), and his wife, Cecilia of Foix. Spanish, Léridan school. First half of 14th century.*

made for Alvaro Rodrigo de Cabrera, count of Urgel, and his wife, Cecilia of Foix, the parents of Ermengol X. The effigy of the small boy has been thought to be that of Ermengol IX, uncle of Ermengol X, because he was the only Cabrera primogenitor to die as a youth. The effigy of the largest sepulchral ensemble resembles the other large tombs, but its style is more elaborate and refined. According to eighteenth-century records, this tomb housed the remains of Ermengol VII (died 1184), who was erroneously thought to have been the founder of the present monastery at Bellpuig de las Avellanes. The effigy reclines on a forward-tilted slab, his hands crossed on his robe, beneath which is a sheathed sword. The head rests upon two tasseled cushions, the upper one wrought with the Urgel arms—checky, gold and black—as traces of color on the stone still indicate. An angel lounging on the top cushion supports the head. A lion crouches at his feet. Behind the effigy, carved from the same large block of stone, are rows of mourners: in front, ladies in long cloaks and knights with swords hanging from their shoulders; in back, figures in hooded mantels. A cleric, standing forward of the crowd, rests his prayer book on the effigy's cushions. Above the mourners, in a separate panel, clerics perform the funeral rite of absolution. Still higher, the soul of the deceased, a small naked figure, is borne to heaven by angels. Three lions support the sarcophagus.

It is not difficult to detect a mixture of styles in this ensemble. The face of the sarcophagus—richly and delicately carved, with Christ in Majesty at the center and the apostles standing in arcaded niches on either side—was carved later than the effigy. The carving of the absolution panel is less fine, and its figures are not in scale with those on the front of the sarcophagus. Moreover, the panel is composed of three fragments—the center from a different source than the two ends.

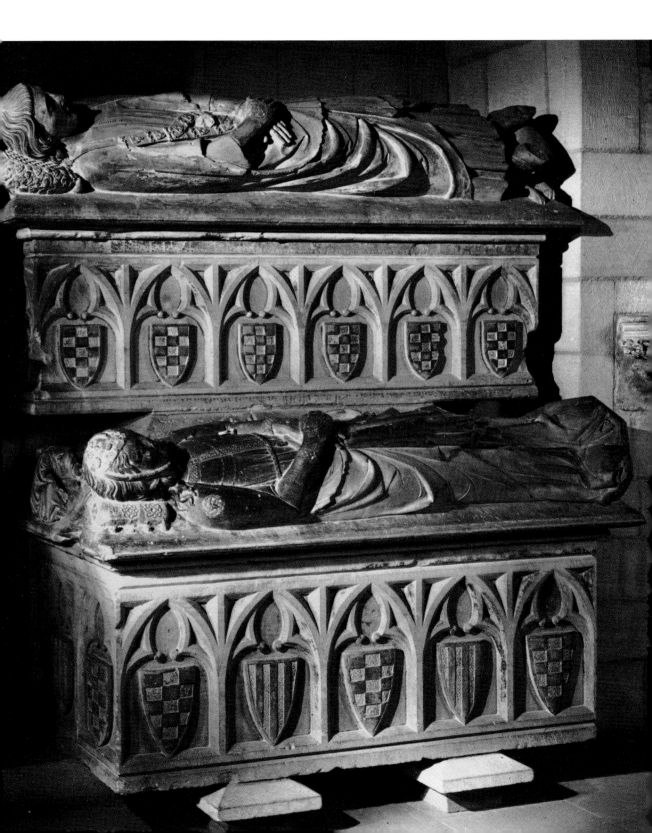

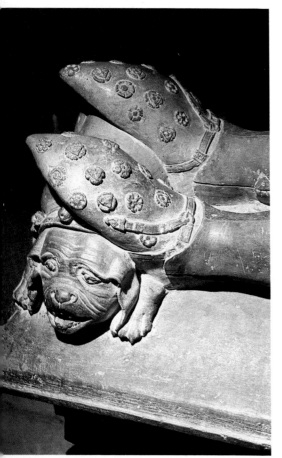

Detail of tomb on opposite page: feet resting on dog.

This tomb is not included in the mid-seventeenth century descriptions of the church. It is mentioned for the first time in the monastery records of the mid-eighteenth century, indicating that it was moved into the church in the intervening century. The Wars of Succession at the turn of the eighteenth century and other events led to the abandonment of Bellpuig, and it was reinhabited in the second decade of the eighteenth century. It may have been during the subsequent renovations that the tomb was assembled from parts of other tombs and used to inter Ermengol VII.

In the double tomb against the opposite wall of the chapel, the sculptor tilted the slabs forward to provide good views of the effigies. Again the heads repose on tasseled cushions decorated with the appropriate arms: checky, gold and black on the upper tomb, the arms of Urgel and Foix on the lower tomb. The arms are repeated in a more elaborate form on the faces of the sarcophagi. On the upper tomb the man's feet rest on a dog rather than the usual lion. An angel steadies the cushion beneath the lady's head on the lower tomb. The lady's feet press against a corbel and the edges of her robe spread out upon it as if she were standing instead of reclining. A griffin, of protective significance in this case, is carved beneath the corbel.

The effigy at the base of the stairs wears a padded surcoat embellished with rosettes and the family arms. A gorget guards his neck and shoulders. His gauntleted hands are crossed upon his sword. Hinged greaves protect his legs. His spurs are fastened with buckled straps. A dog with belled collar rests on his own tilted base in order to support the knight's feet at the proper angle. A small figure—not an angel—seems to invite approval as it holds the decorated cushion beneath the effigy's head. Two dog-like lions support the sarcophagus.

86

Standing free on the floor of the chapel is a lady's tomb slab, believed to have come from the ancient, now ruined, priory of Notre-Dame-du-Bosc, near Neubourg, in Normandy. The date of the slab, indicated by the style of the sculpture and details of the dress, suggests that it may have commemorated Margaret of Gloucester, who married Robert II, baron of Neubourg, when he returned from the Third Crusade. The early seigneurs of Neubourg and their families were benefactors of the priory, and their tombs may well have been placed in the choir of its church. The lady's costume, typical of the thirteenth century, includes a long gown with clasp at the chest, a cloak fastened with a loose cord, and a purse, needle case, and knife hanging from her belt. A doubled cloth strap is drawn tight under her chin, its ends attached to a circlet beneath her veil. Her feet rest against a dog. Angels once guarded the lady at her head and feet.

Tomb of a member of the family of the counts of Urgel, possibly Ermengol X, count of Urgel (died 1314). Spanish, Léridan school. First half of 14th century.

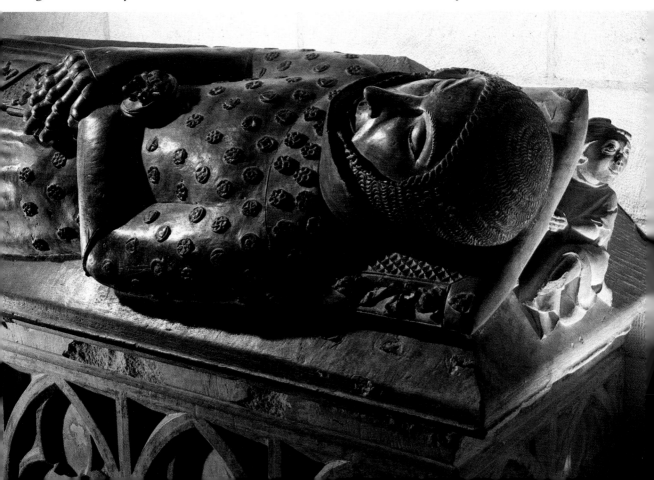

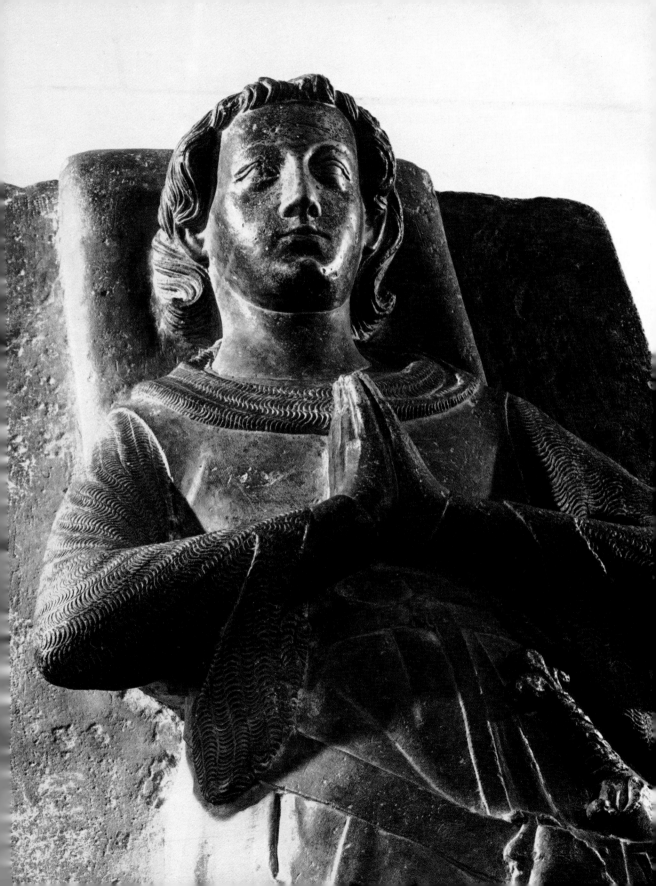

The other slab here is that of the chevalier Jean d'Alluye, who was entombed about 1248 in the abbey he had founded in 1239, La Clarté-Dieu, near Le Mans. The seigneur of several towns in the Loire valley, Jean joined a crusade to the Holy Land in 1240 and brought back a relic of the True Cross. Said to be a model for the Cross of Lorraine, this relic is still preserved in the chapel of the incurables in the hospital of Beaugé. Jean's effigy, a superb example of its type, showing the deceased as youthful and with eyes open, exemplifies the serenity of French thirteenth-century sculpture. At some point in the 1790s, La Clarté-Dieu was vandalized, and later the slab is reported to have been used, face down, to bridge a stream.

In the apse are three very fine sculptures, two Spanish, of the fourteenth century, one French, of the thirteenth century. The female saints are larger than life size and stand beneath stone canopies. Like the tombs of the counts of Urgel, they belong to the Catalan school of Lérida. Enough of their polychrome painting remains to suggest the effect of such sculpture in its own day. The flesh color was tawny, the ridged eyebrows were accented with dark paint, and the greens and reds of the garments were richly bordered with gold.

The bishop, a Burgundian sculpture, has lost little of his mingled dignity and charm, despite severe weathering. Sculptures of this size and quality are rarely away from their architectural settings. This one, found in a garden in Chablis in the 1930s, may once have stood as a trumeau figure at the entrance to a church.

OPPOSITE PAGE: *tomb slab of Jean d'Alluye. About 1248.*

Monumental figure of a bishop. French, Burgundian. Second half of 13th century.

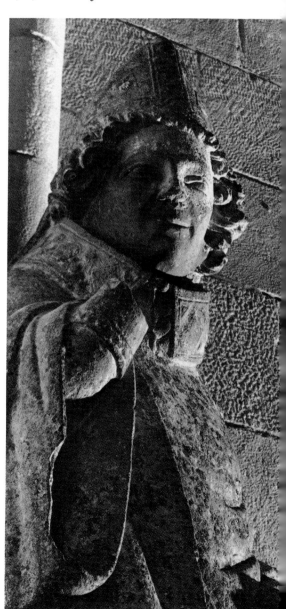

89

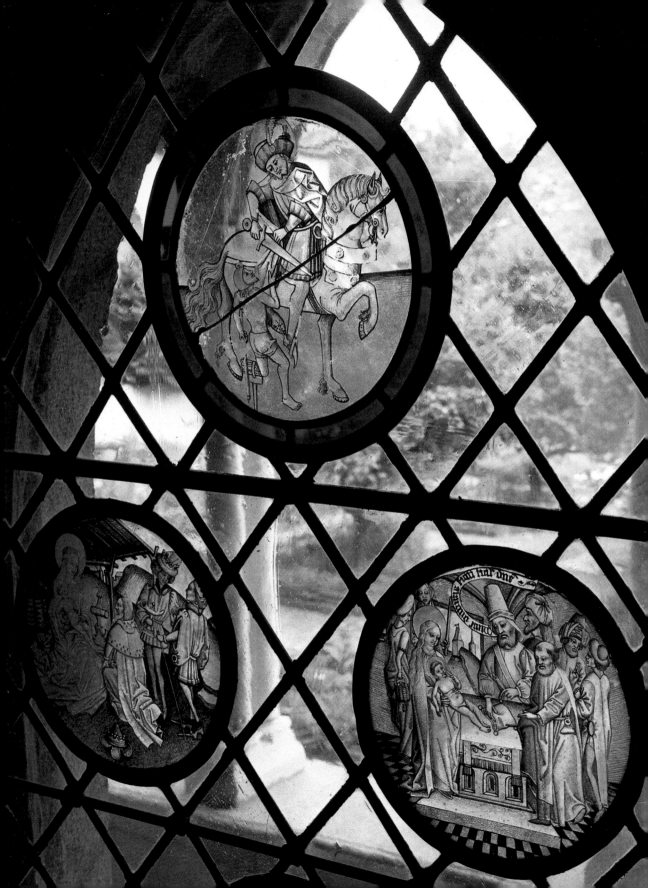

THE BONNEFONT CLOISTER

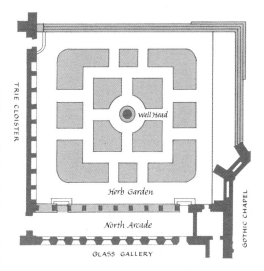

The Cistercian abbey at Bonnefont-en-Comminges, southwest of Toulouse in southern France, was founded in 1136 by monks sent from the "mother abbey" of Morimond, in northern France. The counts of Comminges became the abbey's patrons, and until the middle of the fourteenth century they were buried there. The cloister, built late in the thirteenth or early in the fourteenth century, stood at least until the year 1807, when it was carefully described by a French antiquarian. Fifty years later, little of the structure remained, while architectural elements from the cloister and other parts of the abbey adorned public buildings and gardens for miles around.

From traces of the foundations, still visible in 1934, it could be seen that the cloister, with its four covered walkways, measured some 109 by 78 feet. The two arcades constructed here follow the scheme of arches and parapets

OPPOSITE PAGE: *looking through to the cloister's garden: stained glass. German. Late 15th century.*

North arcade, morning.

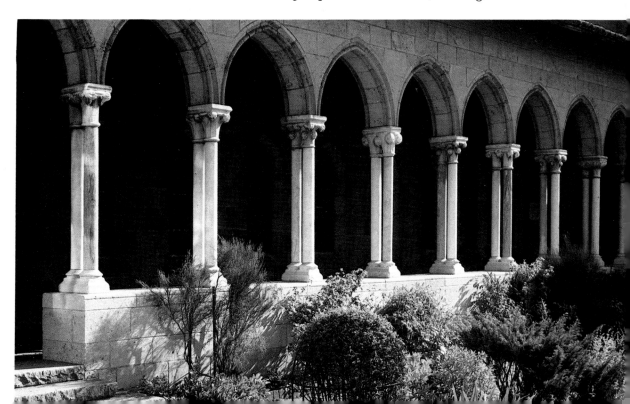

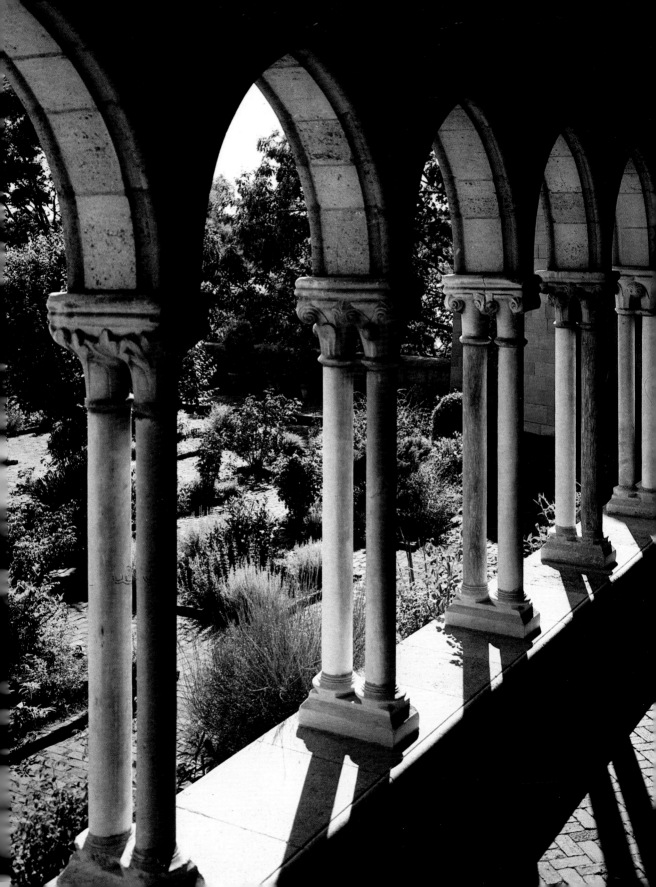

found in fragmentary form at Bonnefont. The simplest of the gray-white marble capitals, placed together in the north arcade, may reflect the severe attitude of the Cistercians toward decorative sculpture. In the east arcade the leaf forms are more naturalistic, and several of the capitals display coats of arms. (A few more of the severely plain capitals have been put to use in the adjoining Trie Cloister, and there, too, will be found four that are carved more elaborately than any here.)

The garden, plotted symmetrically around an Italian wellhead, does not follow a specific model, but in form and planting is meant simply to suggest the look of gardens in medieval paintings and tapestries. Many of the plants and trees that grow here are named in the list that Charlemagne wished to have in the imperial gardens at Aachen. A medlar tree, growing here, is a rarity in the United States but was common in the Middle Ages. It is depicted in the second, third, and fourth of the Unicorn Tapestries. Crushed and mixed with wine, the medlar fruit was believed to be an antidote for poisons.

OPPOSITE PAGE:
North arcade, afternoon.

The wellhead, probably from the region of Venice, was in use for a long time, as can be seen from the rope grooves worn in its rim.

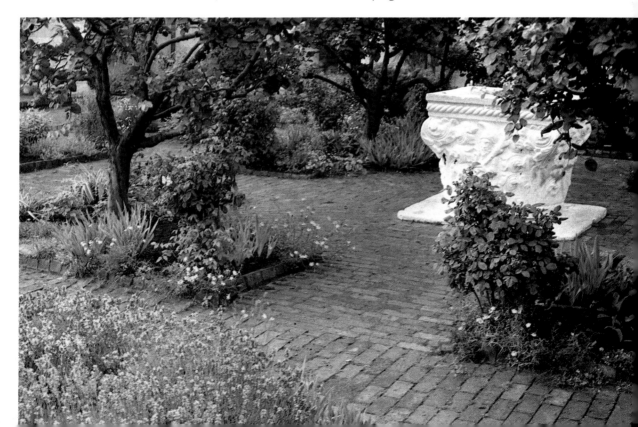

OPPOSITE PAGE: *a glimpse into the Trie Cloister from the Bonnefont Cloister.*
BELOW: *the herb garden of the Bonnefont Cloister, looking southeast.*

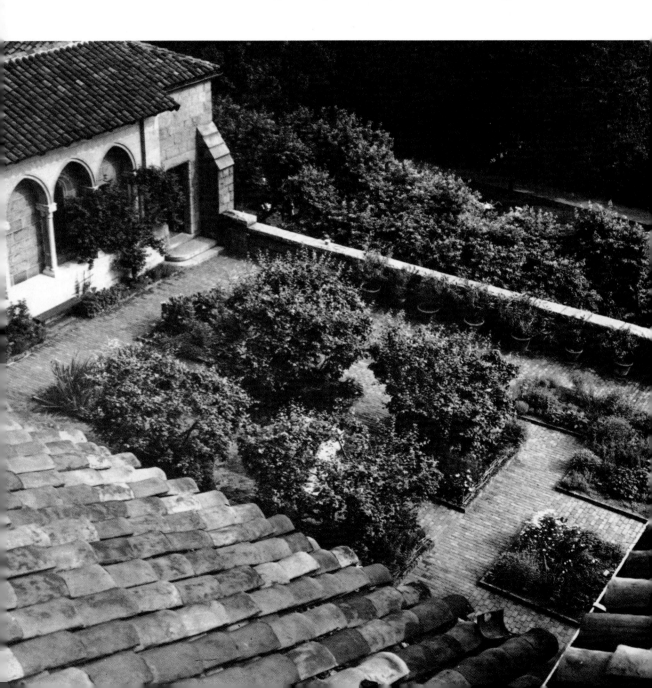

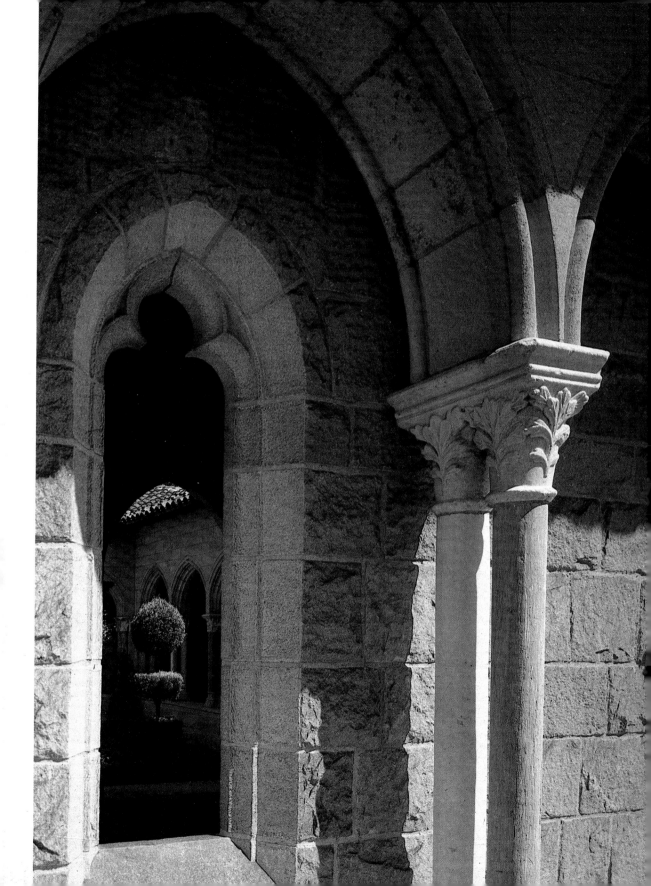

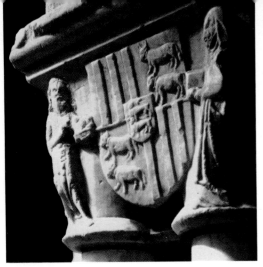
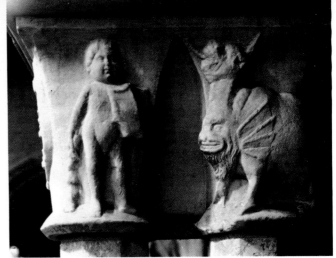

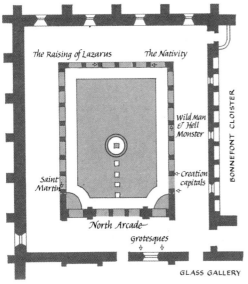

THE TRIE CLOISTER

The white marble capitals that surround the garden came from the long vanished Carmelite convent at Trie-en-Bigorre, west of Toulouse and not far from the site of Bonnefont-en-Comminges. The varicolored marble shafts that support the capitals in the west, south, and east arcades, though old, are not the original shafts.

The carvings, so unlike the stark leaf abstractions in the Bonnefont Cloister, are full of narrative interest. Clearly, they were designed to appeal to the down-to-earth, popular taste of the late Middle Ages. Biblical scenes and popular saints' legends are combined, often on the same capital, with grotesques or coats of arms, a treatment indicative of the growing secularization of the arts. A wild man accosting a hell monster, a head in a fantastic hat, children playing games, and animals in human roles—such fancies repeat the spirit of the drolleries in Gothic manuscripts and the humorous carvings on fifteenth-century choir stalls.

As much as possible with this small group from the original ensemble, the biblical capitals have been installed in order, beginning in the northwest corner with God creating the sun, moon, and stars. Moving south in the west gallery, one comes to the creation of Adam and of Eve, to the angel staying Abraham's hand as he prepares to sacrifice Isaac, and to the saints Matthew and John at work upon their gospels. Around the corner in

West arcade, late afternoon. The arches are modeled on a fragment from the monastery cloister that once existed at Larreule, near Trie.

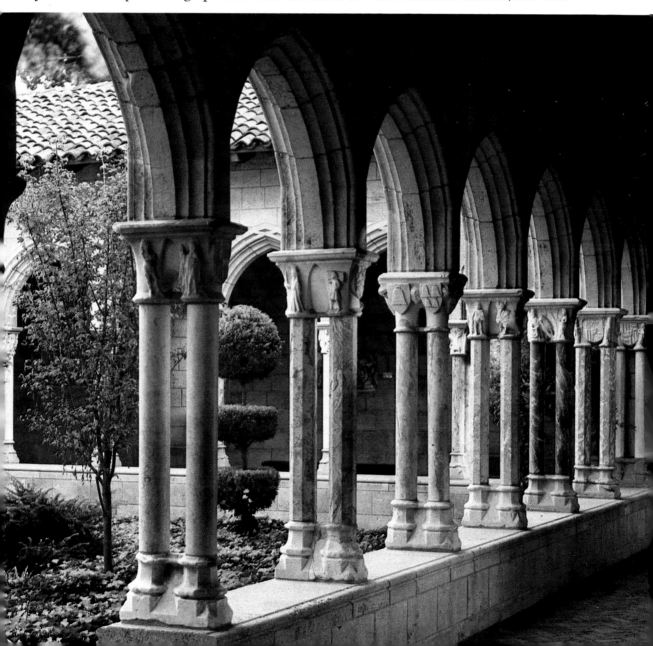

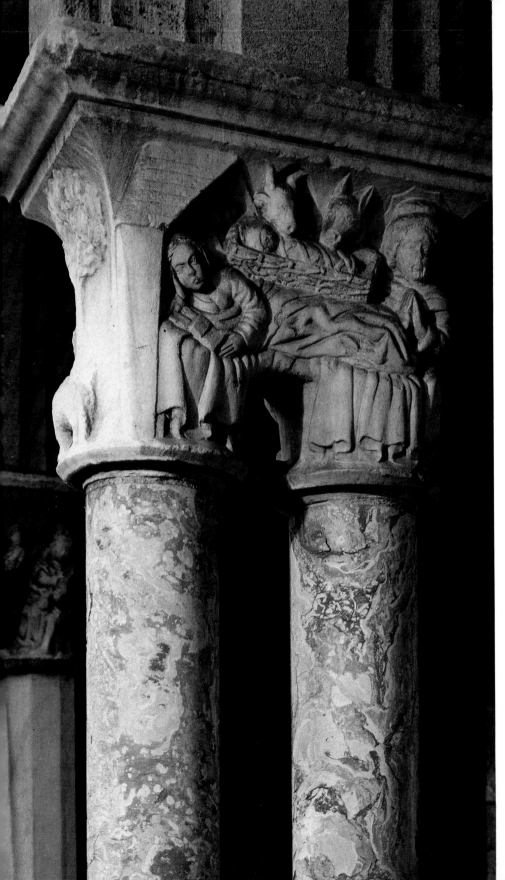

LEFT: *south arcade: the Nativity.*

OPPOSITE PAGE: *above left, south arcade: the Raising of Lazarus; above right, west arcade: a bear spinning with a distaff; below: grotesque beneath the top of a 15th-century French window in the wall of the north walk.*

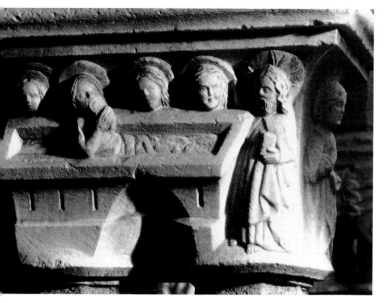

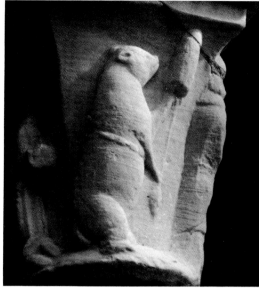

the south gallery are capitals that illustrate the life of Christ: the Annunciation, the Nativity, the Massacre of the Innocents, Satan tempting Christ to turn stones into bread, the Raising of Lazarus, and the Entombment. In the east arcade, among other subjects, are: Saint George slaying the dragon, the stoning of Saint Stephen, Saint Catherine with her wheel, Saint Margaret emerging from the dragon's stomach, the temptation of Saint Anthony, and, last, in the northeast corner, Saint Martin dividing his cloak with the beggar.

The capitals were evidently carved between 1484 and 1490. The first date is indicated by the seventh capital on the west side, which bears the quartered arms of Catherine, queen of Navarre and countess of Bigorre, and her husband, Jean d'Albert, who were married in 1484. The second date is determined by a capital, not in this group, that has an inscription referring to the then living cardinal of Foix, Pierre II, who died in 1490. By 1571 the

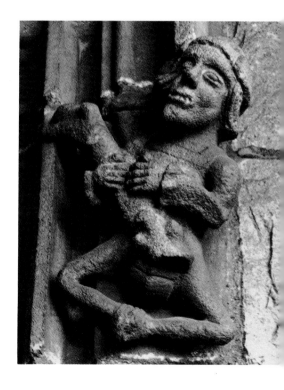

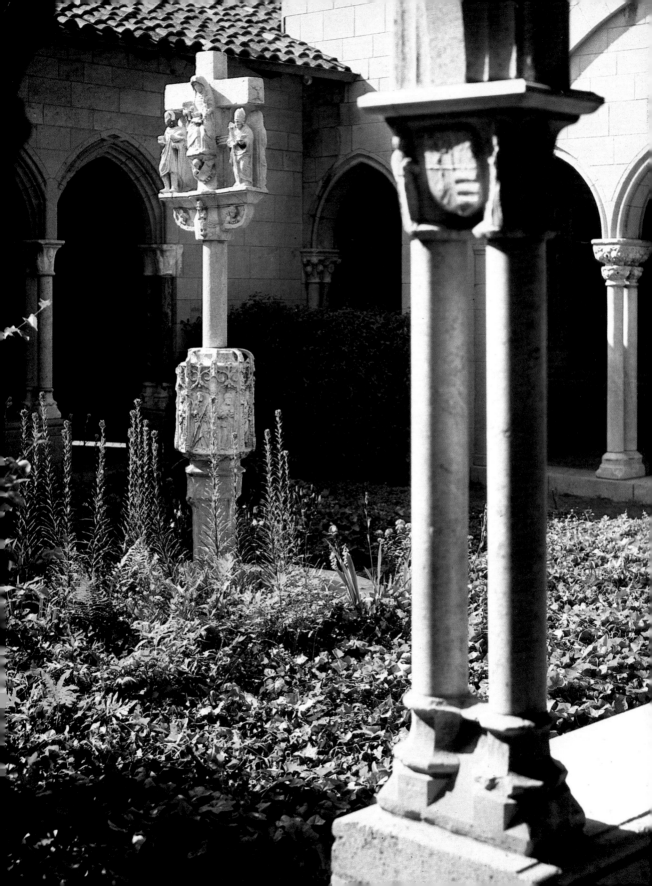

convent had been destroyed by Huguenots. Some of its capitals were set up about 1890 in a public garden in Tarbes, the chief city of the old countship of Bigorre, where they are today. The group here came to this country in 1906.

As for the other features of the Trie Cloister, the leafy gray-white capitals in the north arcade are additional elements from the abbey at Bonnefont, as are four columns and capitals standing free in the east gallery, one of them carved with clusters of grapes. The tiles, roof timbers, and vaulted wooden ceiling were suggested by still existing French structures of the late fifteenth century. At the center of the garden stands a fountain, a composite of two late fifteenth- or early sixteenth-century limestone elements found in the Vosges region of northeastern France.

East arcade, winter.

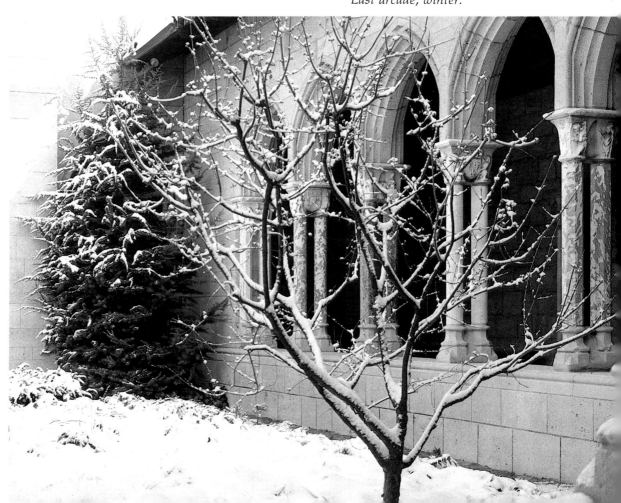

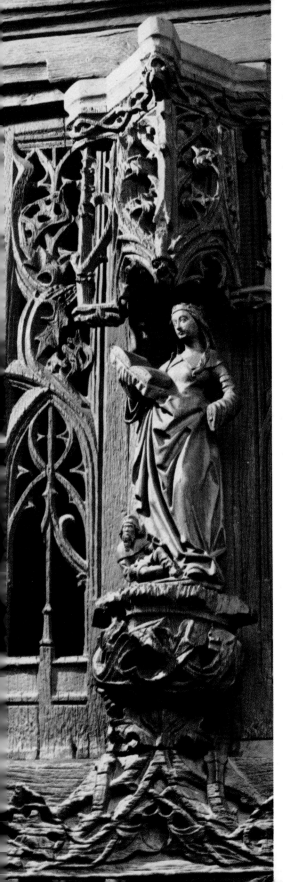

THE ABBEVILLE
WOODWORK AND THE
JUMIEGES PANELS

Reentering the building from the Trie Cloister, one finds medieval woodwork from a half-timbered house that once stood in Abbeville, Picardy, in northwestern France. In northern Europe, where wood was plentiful, it was used extensively for building, often in combination with stucco. These richly carved panels and moldings enclosed a spiral stair that ascended from a courtyard; the adjoining arch spanned a passageway from the courtyard. Above the door on a bracket is a small figure of Saint Catherine, and beside it is a prophet. The late fifteenth- or early sixteenth-century house from which this woodwork was purchased in 1907 was destroyed in World War II.

BEYOND THE STAIRWELL, in a room that opens into The Cloisters' Treasury, is a set of thirty-seven oak panels carved with scenes of the lives of the Virgin and Christ, beginning with the episode of Anna and Joachim being turned away from the Temple and ending with the mourning over the body of Christ at the foot of the Cross. In each panel the action occurs in a tightly constricted space beneath a canopy carved in the flamboyant style. The sharply individualized figures carry out their roles directly and simply, as if they were actors in medieval mystery plays. The styles of at least four different Franco-Flemish craftsmen have been detected in the carvings, which are one of the finest examples of late Gothic wood carving to be found outside Europe.

The panels were acquired early in the nineteenth century by an English connoisseur. It is believed that they were sold to him from what remained, after the Revolution, of the possessions of the former royal abbey of

Details of the Abbeville woodwork.

OPPOSITE PAGE: *Saint Catherine holding a book.*
North French. About 1500.
BELOW: *a prophet. French. 15th or 16th century.*

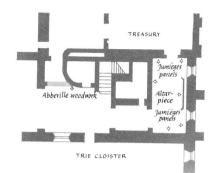

TREASURY

Jumièges panels

Abbeville woodwork

Altar-piece

Jumièges panels

TRIE CLOISTER

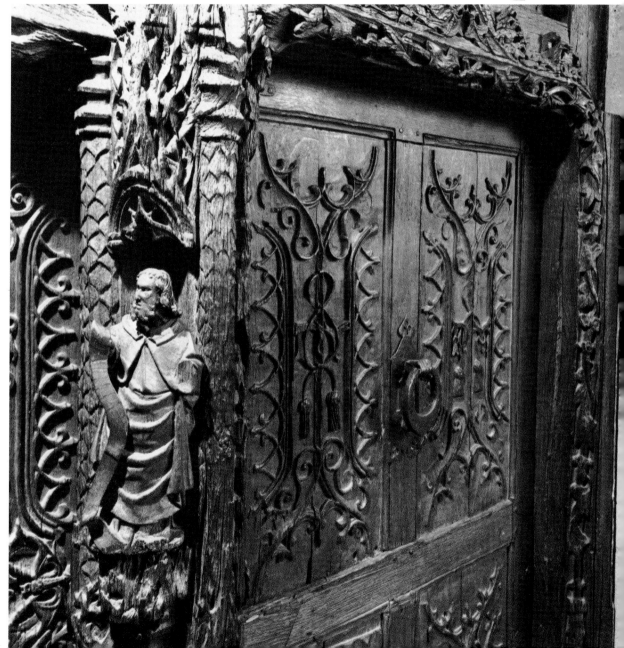

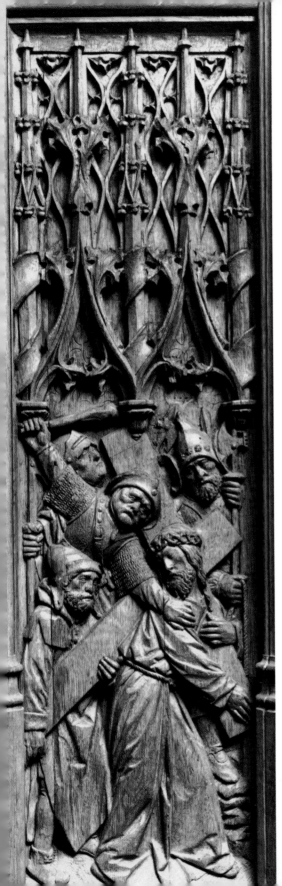

Jumièges, in Normandy. A history of this abbey, compiled by a Benedictine monk about 1764, says that new choir stalls were ordered in 1501. The style of the carving is of this time, and the narrow widths and architectural tops suggest that these panels may have been the backs of the stalls.

PLACED WITH THE Jumièges panels is an altarpiece painted by a follower of Rogier van der Weyden. In the center is the Nativity, and on either side is a scene that, according to legend, took place on the day of the Nativity. On the left the emperor Caesar Augustus, wishing to know whether the world would see the birth of a greater man than he, consults a sibyl. She reveals a vision of an altar in the sky with the Virgin and Child on it, saying, "This child shall be greater than thou." On the right, after bathing and praying, the Magi see the Child in a star, bidding them go to Judea to find the king which is born of a virgin. On the wings of the altarpiece are the Visitation and the Adoration. Looking on from above, surrounded by angels, is God the Father.

In this altarpiece, as in the Jumièges panels, the figures resemble actors in mystery plays. All of them are portrayed without haloes, for example, as human rather than celestial beings. The courtiers who converse behind Augustus are not part of the original legend, but were first introduced in the fifteenth century as characters in mystery plays. And the continuous landscape behind the three principal scenes may be derived from mystery play stage sets, which were sometimes placed side by side out of doors.

OPPOSITE PAGE:
Altarpiece by an unknown master. Mid-15th century.

104

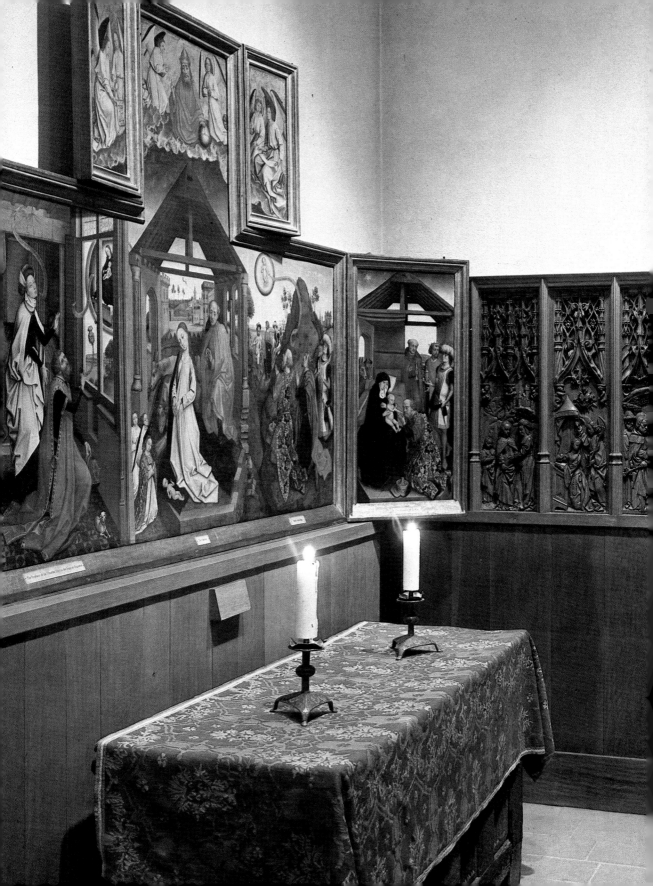

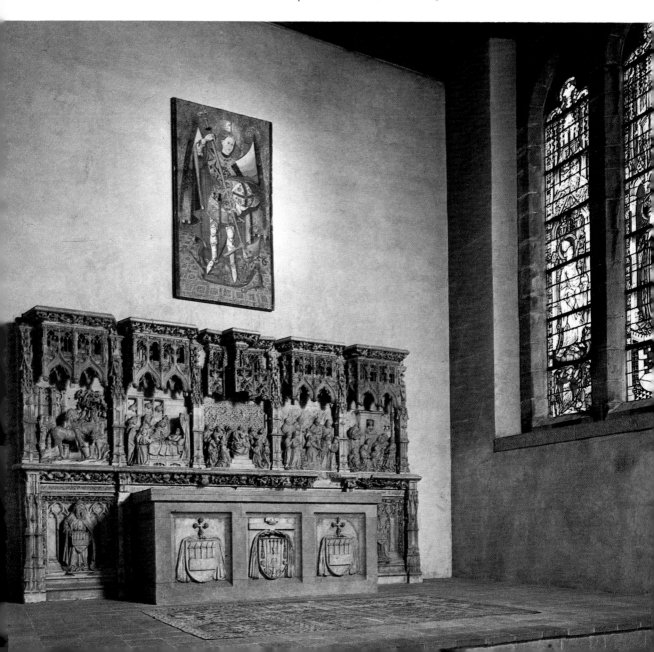

Retable from the palace of the archbishop of Saragossa.
Spanish. Mid-15th century.

THE BOPPARD ROOM

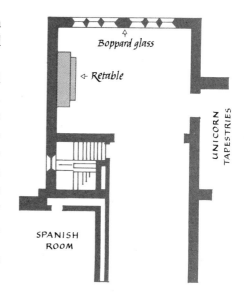

The most dramatic features of the Boppard Room are an intricately carved Spanish retable and six panels of stained glass from the Carmelite church at Boppard-am-Rhein.

The retable, of variegated alabaster, once stood behind the altar in the palace of the archbishop of Saragossa. Traces of paint on the canopied gables indicate that the retable was originally polychromed. Beneath the canopies, with their flamboyant arches and profusion of delicate leaf forms, are scenes from the life of Saint Martin and the life of Saint Thecla; these appear on either side of a panel portraying the day of Pentecost, when the Holy Spirit descended upon the apostles in tongues of fire. Figures beneath the retable hold shields bearing the arms of Don Dalmacio de Mur, who became archbishop of Saragossa in 1434.

Alabaster, quarried in the Ebro valley in northern Spain, is a compact stone, ideal for the realization of fine detail. The sculptor of this work was interested in narration and realism, and like other Spanish artists of the mid-fifteenth century, he was influenced by works of art then being made in Flanders, where objects of everyday life were often introduced in religious scenes. In his representation of Christ visiting the future Saint Martin in a dream, bringing with him the piece of cloak that Martin presented to the beggar, the sculptor has put valanced curtains around the sleeper to protect him from drafts, and has shown his cat and his shoes beneath the bed. In the scene where Thecla listens to the preaching of Saint Paul from a window of her home, she rests her arms upon a plump, tasseled pillow.

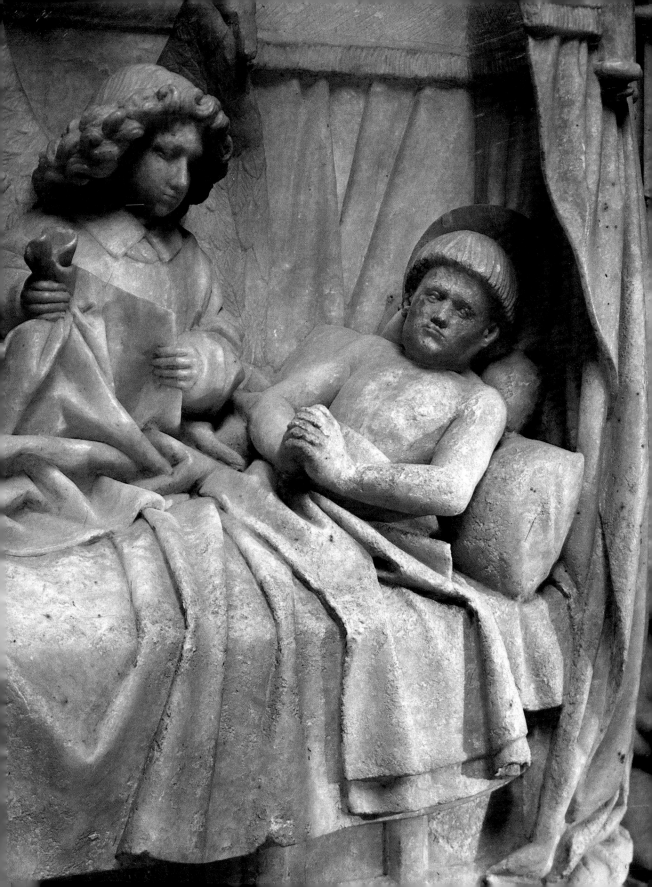

Detail of the retable: in a dream, Martin of Tours is visited by Christ. An angel holds the half of the cloak that Martin cut for the beggar. Soon after this dream Martin decided to be baptized.

Another detail of the retable: after her conversion, Thecla refused to marry the man betrothed to her. For this, she was condemned to be burnt, but God caused a cloud to pour down rain on her pyre.

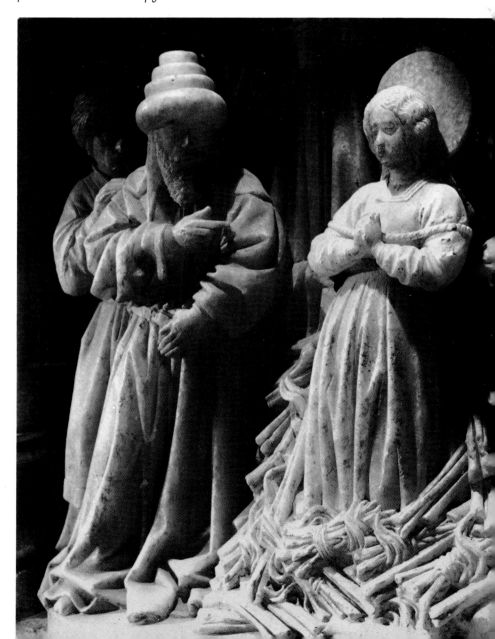

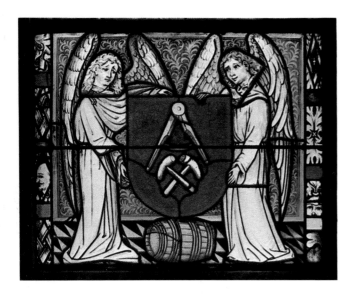

OPPOSITE PAGE: *two of the Boppard stained-glass lancets. German, Rhenish, 1440–1447. Saint Catherine with the wheel and sword of her martyrdom, and Saint Dorothea receiving from the Christ Child a basket of three roses from the celestial garden.*

At the base of the Saint Catherine lancet angels display the arms of the coopers' guild, of which Catherine was the patron.

Even more elaborate than the canopies of the retable are the vaulted structures that surround the saints in the adjacent Boppard glass. These six lancets, placed three over three, originally constituted a single tall window, made and installed between 1440 and 1447 in the nave of the Boppard church. The white glass used so extensively in the compositions recalls the silvery tones of panel paintings produced at that period in Cologne, sixty miles down the Rhine from Boppard. Likewise reminiscent of Cologne painting are the slender, elongated figures in their trailing drapery and the sweet faces of the female saints. The Rhine acted as an artery, transmitting artistic influences from centers of production to outlying areas.

After Napoleon's invasion of the Rhineland and the subsequent secularization of church property, the glass at Boppard was gradually stripped away. Not only are these lancets the most brilliant ensemble of late Gothic stained glass in the United States, they are the only ones from the great series once at Boppard to have survived intact.

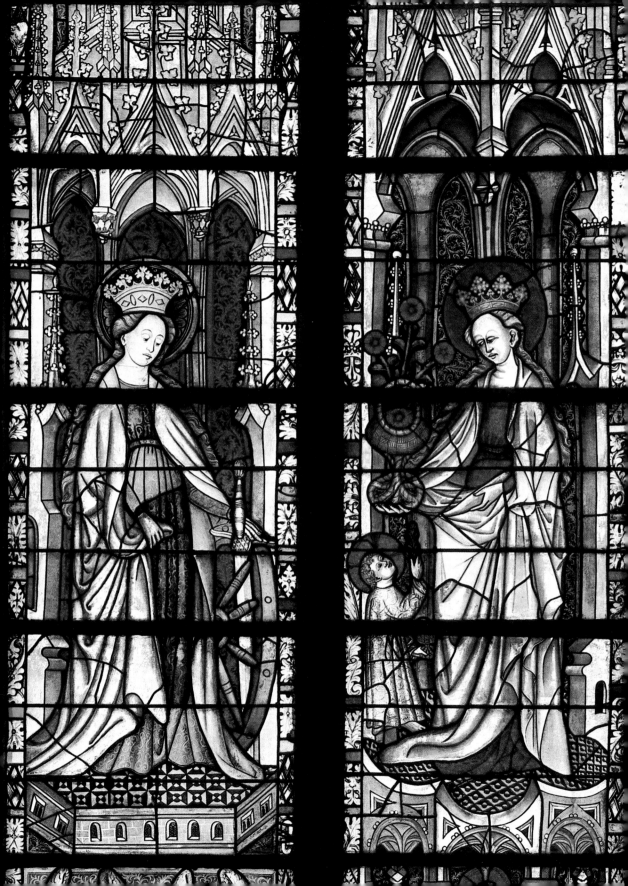

THE SPANISH ROOM

Spanish ceiling of painted pine, decorated with interlacing stems bearing leaves and fruit. 15th century. In the frieze at the bottom are hunting scenes and unidentified coats of arms, probably a later addition. The 15th-century bronze chandelier with a kneeling angel at the top is probably Flemish.

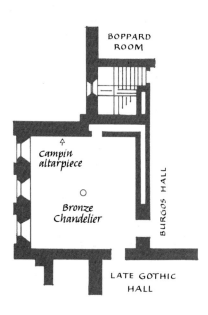

Though furnished to simulate a domestic interior, the Spanish Room has none of the grand scale of the Unicorn Tapestries Room, where the monumental fireplace and armorial glass at the window give the impression of a castle hall. Here, the setting is more intimate, and the objects—including even a birdcage—are of the type made for the everyday use and pleasure of prosperous middle-class people of the fifteenth century.

The room takes its name from its Gothic ceiling. Of red pine coated thinly with gesso and painted, it came from a small *palacio* at Illescas, halfway between Madrid and Toledo, where it is said to have been in a bedroom occupied by Francis I of France when he was a prisoner of Emperor Charles V in 1525–26.

The chandelier, probably Flemish, must once have lit a room for an important family, since candles were a luxury in the Middle Ages. The chandelier was fashioned with great care, the pieces cast separately and each of the nine branches given an assembly mark corresponding to a mark on the central shaft. The entire surface was tooled, and the rough spots on the bronze were smoothed before it was polished to a high gleam.

Commanding the view of the room is the Annunciation altarpiece by Robert Campin, often called the Mérode altarpiece after the family that owned it in the nineteenth century. The painting contains versions of many of the furnishings in the Spanish Room: the beamed ceiling, the high-backed bench of oak and walnut with dog and lion finials, the bronze laver with two spouts and chain for suspension in a niche, the candlestick and majolica vase

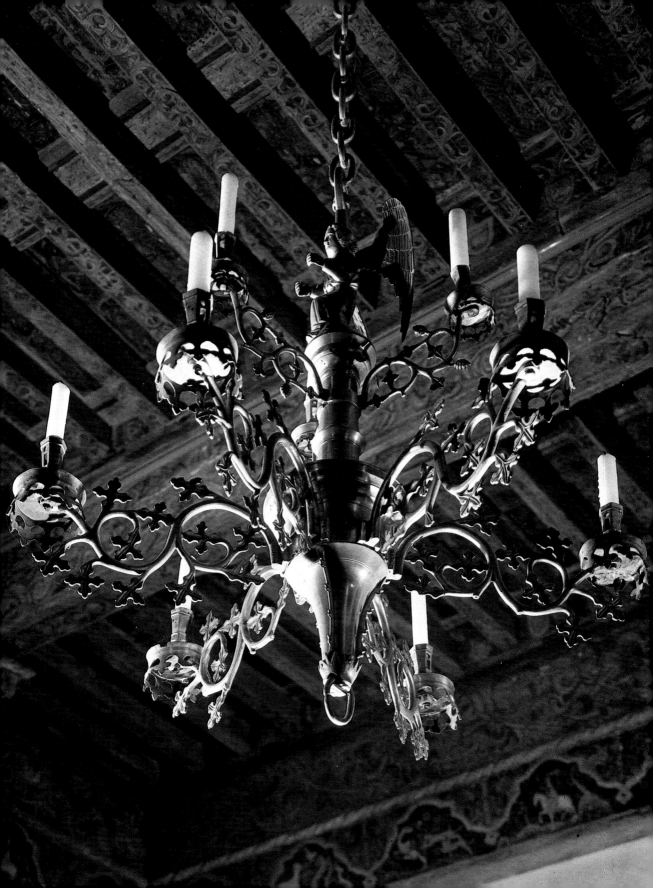

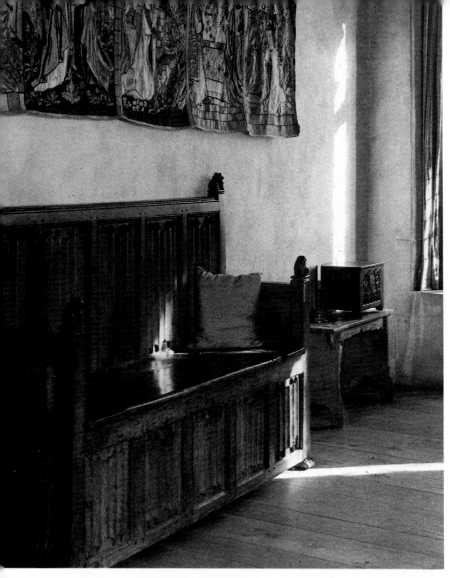

Walnut bench with linen-fold panels and finials in the form of lions and dogs. French or Spanish. About 1500. Compare the bench in the center panel of Campin's altarpiece.

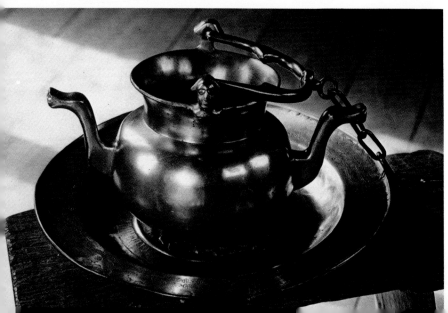

A bronze laver with bird- or reptile-head spouts and handle fitted into sockets in the form of human heads. Flemish. 15th century. Compare Campin's laver.

on the table, the wall bracket with candle. Campin was mentioned in 1406 as a master painter of Tournai, in southern Belgium. This altarpiece, probably painted about 1425, is in the new Flemish technique of oil colors on wood panels. It is also innovative in its pictorial approach, for the angel's Annunciation to Mary, which up to this time would have been shown occurring in a portico or an ecclesiastical setting, is set in a bourgeois living room of the artist's own time and place.

In countries where there was a strong central government—as in France—and a tradition of feudalism, with lord above vassal, the patrons of the arts were mainly the royalty and nobility. The Nine Heroes Tapestries, for example, made less than fifty years before Campin's altarpiece, were commissioned by or for a brother of

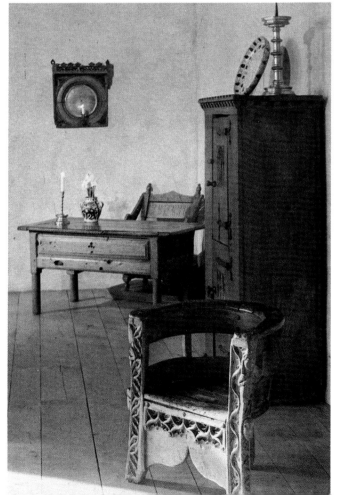

Household furnishings of the 15th or early 16th century. On the table, a German brass candlestick and an Italian majolica jug. On the chest, a large pricket candlestick and a Spanish lusterware plate. Beyond the table is a reflector designed to increase the illumination of a candle.

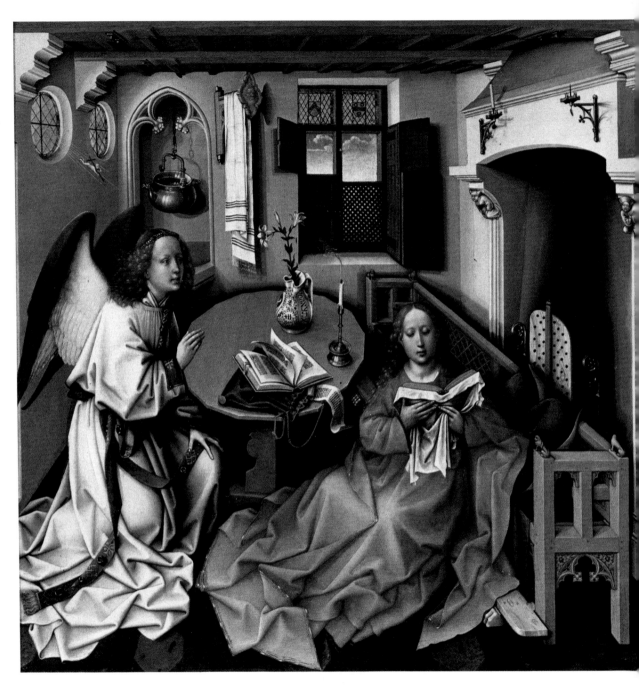

The central panel of the Altarpiece of the Annunciation,
by Robert Campin of Tournai. About 1425.

the king of France. But in the Low Countries, where there was little political unity, numerous independent and active towns determined the pattern of life. In these trade centers there arose a new middle class, the leading members of which could afford to commission works quite as fine as those made for the nobility elsewhere. Such a person was Mr. Ingelbrecht of Malines (Mechelen), in Belgium, for whom, presumably, Campin created this altarpiece. The arms in the left-hand window in the central panel are Ingelbrecht's, and it is he who is portrayed kneeling with his wife outside the Virgin's door.

Although this Flemish work was produced little more than a decade after another superb work by Netherlandish painters to be seen in The Cloisters, the *Belles Heures* made for the duke of Berry (p. 136), an extraordinary change in artistic outlook has taken place. The world that the Limbourg brothers depicted in the duke's book of hours is elegant, courtly, almost ethereal. Campin's world, like his patron, is more prosaic, with directness replacing refinement. The domestic objects in his painting are not only real, but tangible, their solidity enhanced by shadows and reflections of light on surfaces. In effect, the *Belles Heures* paintings epitomize an earlier tradition, while Campin's painting anticipates the future.

Noteworthy is his representation of the donor. Earlier, the donor of a painting was apt to be shown small in size, a subordinate presence in the composition. Here, in a lifelike manner, he is as large as the other figures, and he takes an active part in the drama, looking on with his wife as the angel appears to Mary, while she, as yet unaware of the angel's presence, continues with her reading.

But although Campin clearly rejoices in his ability to show us objects of the real world, painting each of them to emphasize its particular beauty of form and texture, he is guided primarily by the symbolic needs of his story. His bronze laver is present as a symbol of Mary's purity, like

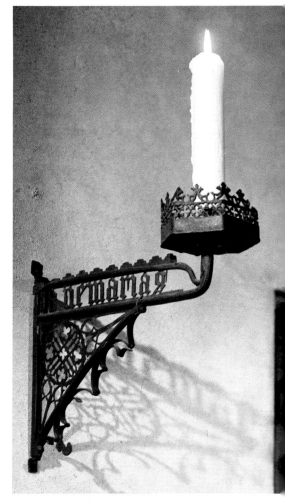

A wrought-iron candle bracket like those on Campin's fireplace. The top of the bracket is pierced to read Ave Maria G[ratia Plena].

117

Right-hand panel of the altarpiece: Joseph in his shop.

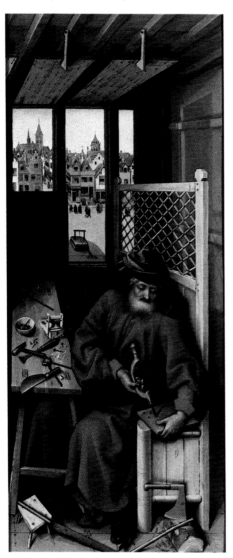

the Madonna lily in the vase—which occurred so prominently in the Unicorn in Captivity tapestry. The candle on the table is a symbol of Christ; the candlestick represents the Virgin who bore him. The rays of the sun entering the window give visual form to the medieval allegory of the perpetual virginity of Mary, which Saint Bernard explains thus: "Just as the brilliance of the sun fills and penetrates a glass window without damaging it, and pierces its solid form with imperceptible subtlety, neither hurting it when entering nor destroying it when emerging . . . the word of God, the splendor of the Father, entered the virgin chamber and then came forth from the closed womb." Campin demonstrates Mary's essential humility by seating her on the floor instead of on the bench. The finials of the bench are also meaningful, for the dog was a widely understood symbol of fidelity in the Middle Ages, while the lion, merciful as well as courageous, was a symbol of Christ.

In his workshop Joseph has made what are thought to be two mousetraps (one of them already set on the window ledge). As Saint Augustine explained: "The cross of the Lord was a mousetrap for the Devil, the bait by which he would be caught was the Lord's death." And we see that the Child, borne on the entering rays of light in the main scene, already carries the cross of the Lord. His martyrdom is further represented by the red rose growing on the wall of the donor's garden.

When these panels were cleaned some years ago, it was found that the likeness of the donor's wife was painted over the grass of the background and that the coats of arms in the living-room windows were also early alterations. One interpretation of this overpainting is that Ingelbrecht was still a bachelor when he commissioned the triptych, and had the additions made after his marriage. The coat of arms in the right-hand window is thought to be that of the Calcum family.

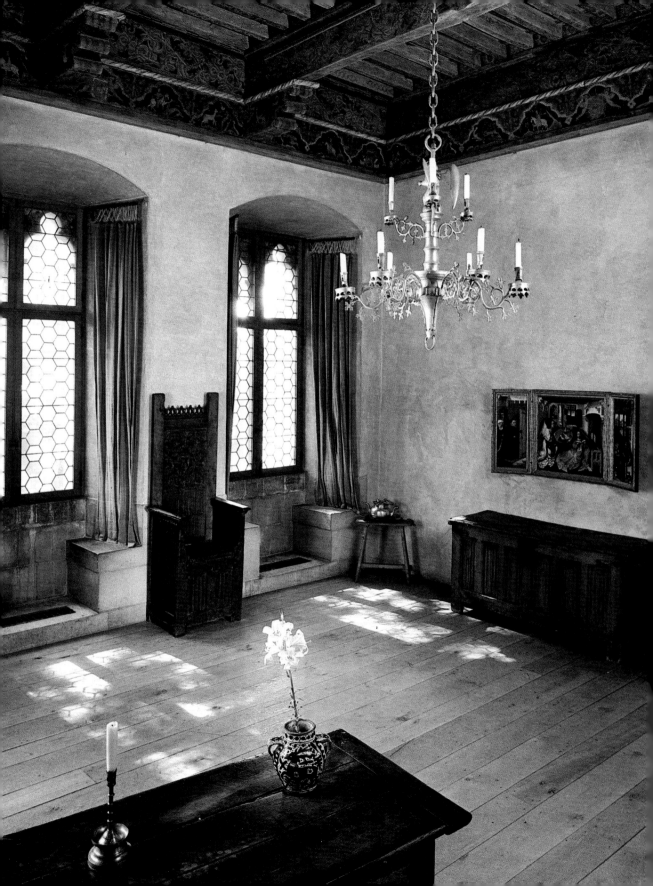

SCULPTURES, METALWORK, AND OTHER OBJECTS

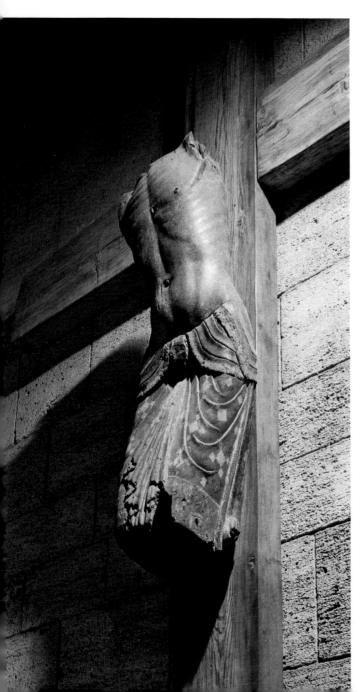

Throughout the rooms and halls of The Cloisters are outstanding works of art not associated with a particular architectural setting and therefore not always exhibited in the same location. The interested visitor will be rewarded for his efforts in searching out the items presented below, selected from a number of important objects not discussed in the previous pages.

Torso of Christ. This wood carving, a part of a Crucifixion, came from Lavaudieu, in central France, where it was made in the third or fourth decade of the twelfth century. The figure is an extraordinarily fine example of Romanesque sculpture in the style of Auvergne, with the graceful curves of the body simplified and the delicate, flattened folds of the loincloth falling in a series of soft zigzags. The sensitive modeling of the body reveals an interest in realistic expression that points to the Gothic style in sculpture. In order that the quality of the carving itself would not be hidden, the wood was given only thin coats of gesso and paint. Originally, the loincloth was blue, with appliqué ornaments of clustered squares, probably of precious metal. Later, the blue was painted over with scarlet and green, and the ornamental squares were outlined in black and yellow.

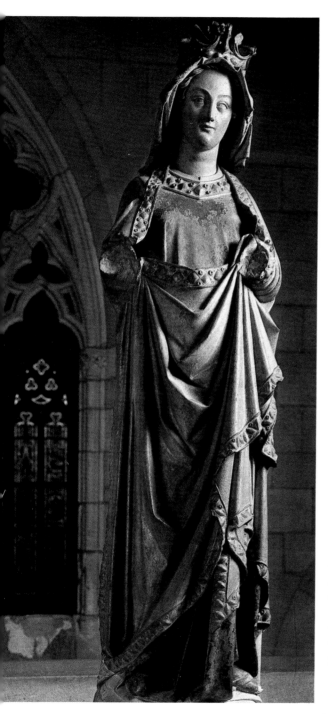

Virgin from Strasbourg Cathedral.
Of polychromed sandstone, the flat back left unfinished, this statue once appeared with others on the cathedral's great choir screen, which was completed shortly after 1250. Two angels supported the Virgin's veil while two more flew above her head. The Child did not rest on his mother's arm in the usual way but sat upon a rosebush at her side. These details of the severely vertical composition are preserved in a drawing of the choir screen that was made about 1660. The screen itself was taken down in 1682 to make space for the ceremonial changes introduced by Louis XIV.

With majestic yet simple grace the Strasbourg Virgin expresses the noble ideal of High Gothic sculpture. In contrast to the transcendental images of the Virgin to be seen in the Langon Chapel, this Virgin, though regal enough, seems more sympathetically aware of mankind's existence.

Virgin and Child. From the Ile-de-France, this polychromed limestone sculpture affords an excellent comparison with the Strasbourg Virgin. Both interpret the Virgin as Queen of Heaven—sovereign, gracious, and serene—but this fourteenth-century statue was designed to be freestanding. Accordingly, its composition was not

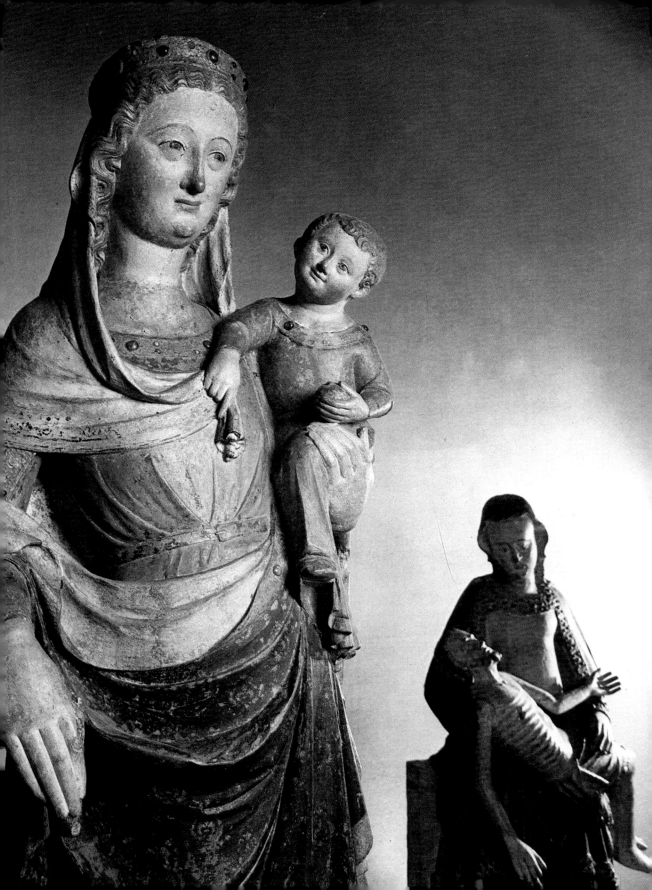

determined by a flat architectural setting. The body sways in a graceful S-curve, in a stance any mother might take to hold her child in her arm. The draperies are soft and pliant, revealing the form of the body beneath.

The statue is in an extraordinary state of preservation. The paint and gilding are almost intact, and most of the cabochon stones are still present in the crown and borders of the garments.

(In the background is a German Pietà of the fourteenth century.)

South German Pietà. No subject was more congenial to medieval piety than the sorrowing figure of Mary with her dead son. The subject is usually called by its Italian name, perhaps because Italian Pietàs, though not the earliest examples, are the best known. The idea seems to have had its origin in the contemplations of mystics for whom the Pietà became an image of devotion quite separate from the usual scenes of the Passion. In this example in painted and gilded wood the body of Christ is full-size, and Mary has assumed an expression of tenderness, rather than the look of intense grief she wears in earlier Pietàs. Our example, made around 1435, came from the convent of Himmelspforten, near Würzburg.

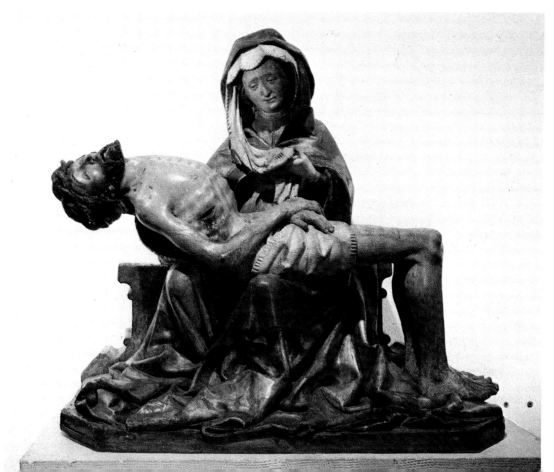

King Melchior. In the Middle Ages, particularly in the Netherlands and Germany, the kings who brought the Christ Child gifts of gold, frankincense, and myrrh were thought to have descended from the three sons of Noah, and thus to represent the three races of mankind. In The Cloisters' group, carved about 1490, Melchior is the Asian king. He kneels to present his gift, while the others, Caspar and Balthazar, stand waiting their turn. The three nearly life-size figures of lindenwood were once part of the high altar in the convent of Lichtenthal, in Baden-Baden.

Kneeling Virgin from a Nativity group. Carved in willow and polychromed and gilded, this serene yet moving figure

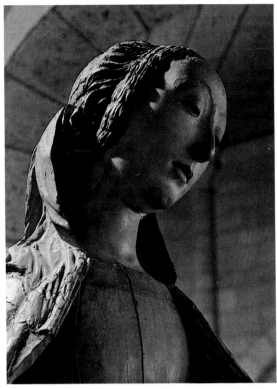

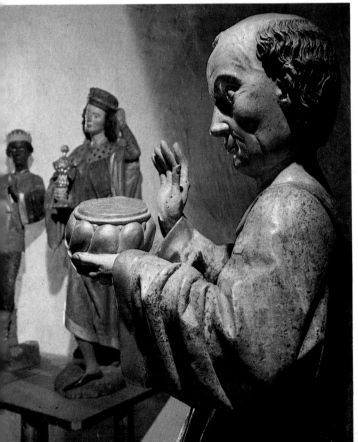

was probably made about 1475 by Paola Aquilana, a sculptor of the Abruzzi school, in central Italy. Two other sculptures by him are known. Although the costume and coiffure might be those of any stylish, sophisticated woman of the late fifteenth century, the attitude of humility and adoration clearly shows that the figure is intended to be Mary, gazing adoringly at her newborn son.

Three saints by Tilman Riemenschneider. Unpainted sculptures, utilizing the natural texture of the plain wood, began to appear during the late fifteenth century, at the end of the Middle Ages. A number by Riemenschneider, one of the

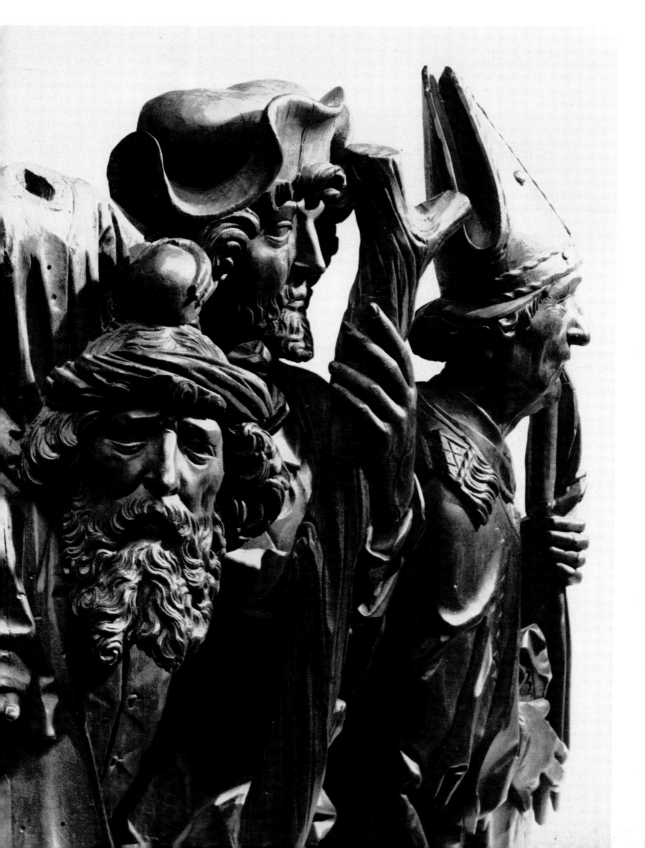

great masters of German sculpture, are known. Here, in a characteristic combination of skilled realism and intense emotional expression, he has portrayed Saint Christopher bearing the Christ Child, Saint Eustace as a young knight, and Saint Erasmus in his bishop's vestments, holding his crozier in one hand, a fragment of a windlass, his symbol, in the other. These three saints belong to a group known in Germany as the *Nothelfer,* or "Helpers in Need." The sculpture, small in size, was part of a commission in 1494 for a hospital dedicated to the Nothelfer in a suburb of Würzburg.

Saint James the Greater. In 1486 Isabel of Castile, the patron of Columbus, commissioned an elaborate alabaster tomb for her parents, Juan II of Castile and Isabel of Portugal; it was placed in the Carthusian monastery of Miraflores in Burgos. The sculptor, Gil Siloe, employed assistants who were responsible for many of the monument's figures, but this statuette of the patron saint of Spain must surely have been by him alone. The carving of the entire piece, especially the fine details of the hands and face, is masterful. Portrayed as a pilgrim, the saint wears the pilgrim's gourd hanging from his staff; a hat adorned with a cockleshell and the crossed staffs worn by pilgrims to Santiago de Compostela; and another cockleshell clasping his mantle.

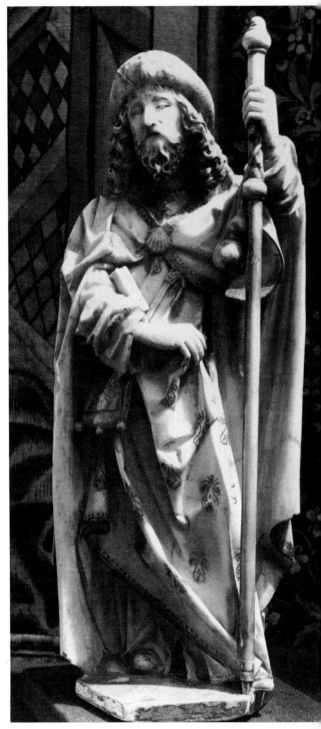

The Antioch chalice. This very early liturgical vessel, a plain cup of silver within an elaborate openwork cup of silver gilt on a knobbed stem, no doubt belonged to a wealthy parish—presumably the parish at Antioch, in Syria, near where it was reportedly discovered in 1910. Among the scrolling grapevines are representations of Christ, one instructing his disciples, the other enthroned above an eagle with wings outstretched, signifying the Resurrection. The vines ("I am the true vine," Jesus said) and a basket of what may represent loaves of bread are in accord with the chalice's Eucharistic function. Soon after the chalice came to light, it was suggested that the inner cup was the Holy Grail, but the workmanship and design mark it as a creation of the sixth century.

Ciborium bowl. All that remains of a twelfth-century ciborium, or container for the consecrated host, is this silver bowl, probably made in either northern France or England. The base and the domed cover with finial have not survived. The decoration is carried out in silver, silver gilt, and niello—a contrasting black compound of sulfur, copper, silver, and lead. Though it is small in actual size, the figure of a man entwined in stylized branches as he struggles to escape from dragons is monumental in effect, with all the vitality to be found in the finest of Romanesque art.

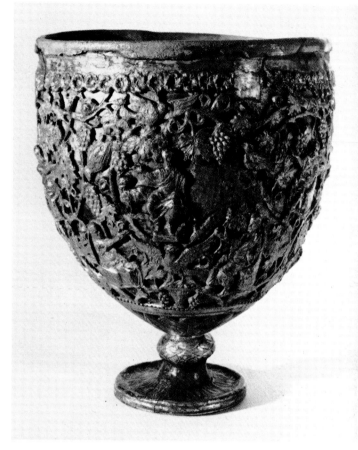

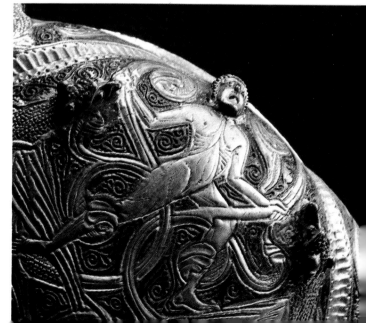

Flabellum. Among the most spectacular of liturgical objects, flabellums, fans of metal, were placed on altars or carried by deacons in processions. Ceremonial rather than functional, they were descended from fans of parchment and feathers used in early medieval times during the Mass to "keep away the small animals that fly about, that they may not come near the cups."

The Cloisters' flabellum, decorated with exceptional richness in silver-gilt filigree set with jewels, polished tin, champlevé enamel, and gilt bronze, has parallels in goldsmiths' work made around 1200 in the region of the Rhine and Meuse rivers. The central boss is hinged, opening to reveal a compartment that once held a relic.

Reliquary shrine of the Virgin and Child. In the form of a miniature altar-piece, with hinged wings at either side, this fourteenth-century shrine of silver gilt and translucent enamel was made in Paris around 1345. It is believed to have been made for Queen Elizabeth of Hungary, and possibly to have been bequeathed by her to the convent of the Poor Clares in Budapest, which she founded in 1334. The little scenes on the wings, front and back, are of a jewel-like brilliance, resembling stained glass, and a number of the architectural details are reminiscent of Gothic churches, notably the trefoil arches and the ribbed vaulting above the seated Madonna and her attendant angels. Since most of the scenes on the wings have to do with the infancy of Christ, it seems probable that the angels once displayed relics associated with the Nativity in their small windowed boxes.

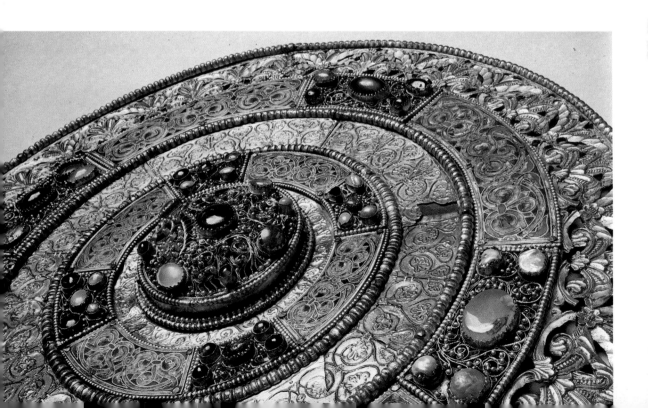

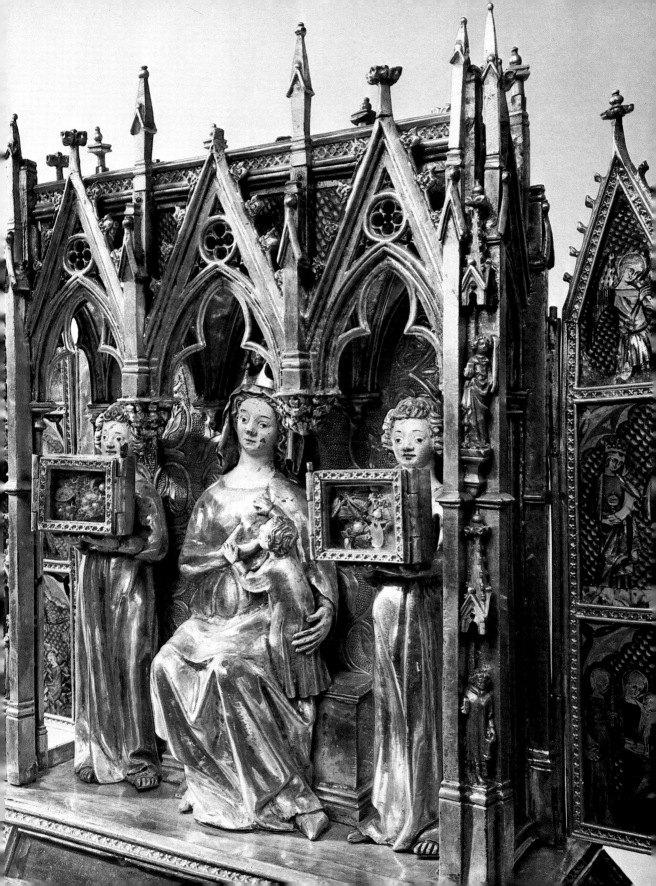

Silver-gilt beaker ("Monkey Cup").
The coloring of this beaker, which was probably made for the Burgundian court around 1425–50, is called "painted" enamel, because the material was applied freely over the metal, without the grooves that separate the colors in champlevé enameling or the incised patterns that provide guidelines for the application of translucent enamels. Inside the beaker two monkeys, with their hounds, pursue two stags. One monkey has a hunting horn, the other a bow and arrow. The chase occurs against a stylized forest with a cloud band at the top. On the exterior, thirty-five monkeys rob a sleeping peddler of his wares and his clothing, and disport themselves with their

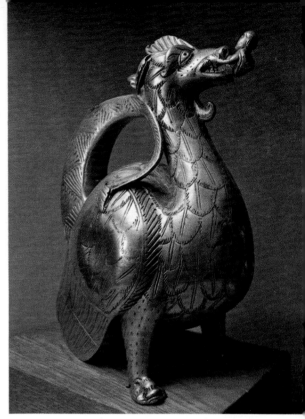

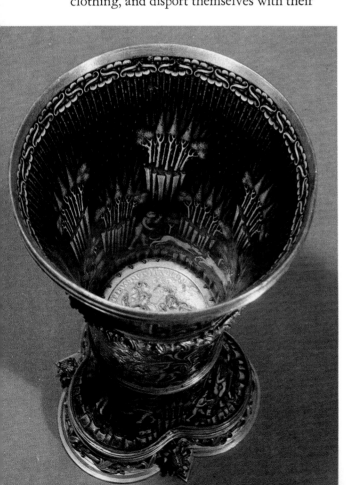

prizes in the beaker's elegant foliage scrolls. The theme of the mischievous monkeys and the unlucky peddler was widely appreciated in the fifteenth and sixteenth centuries. This rare and beautiful beaker, the work of Flemish or Franco-Flemish artists, would hardly have been used on ordinary occasions, for its enamel is virtually brittle glass.

Aquamaniles. Made of bronze in imaginative, often seemingly playful forms, aquamaniles held water for the washing of priests' hands before the celebration of the Mass, and in households for the washing of hands at meals. The two illustrated hint at the individuality of the designs. The dragon swallowing a man curves his tail over his winged body to make the handle. The water issued from a hole beneath the man's head. Of German manufacture, this aquamanile dates from the twelfth or early thirteenth century. The mounted falconer, who once carried a falcon on his gloved wrist, was made in the first half of the thirteenth century. At the top of the horse's head is a square opening, originally hinged, for filling the vessel; the water poured from the horse's mouth.

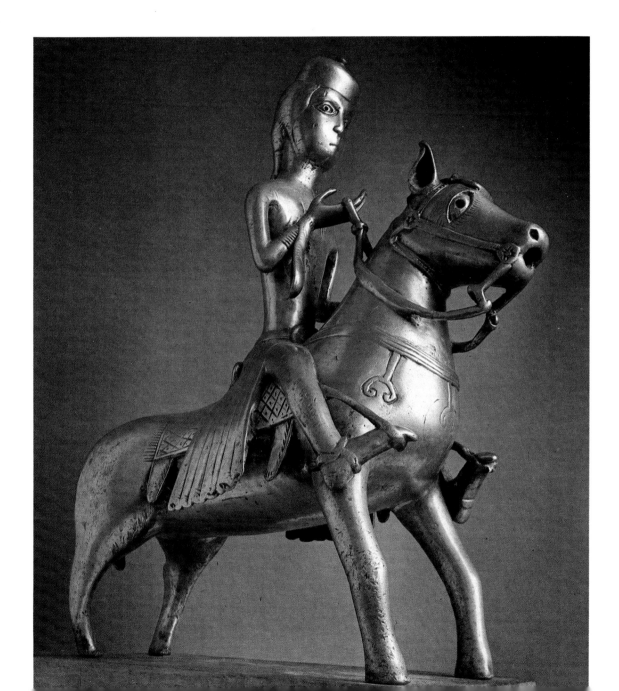

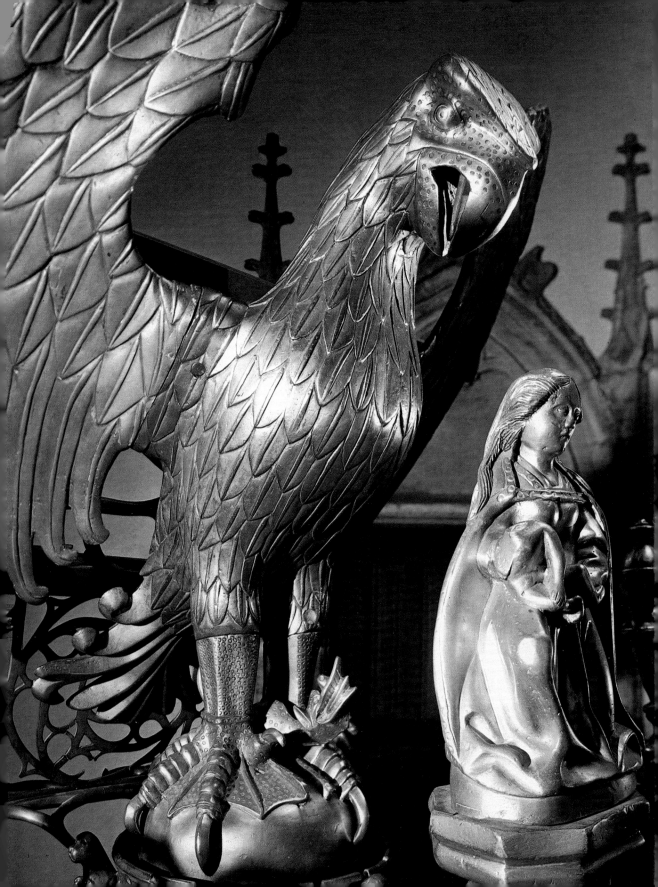

Eagle lectern. Assembled from pieces cast separately, this monumental work in brass was made about 1500, possibly by the Belgian metal caster Aert van Tricht the Elder. Well over six feet in height, the lectern rests upon couchant lions and is topped by an eagle holding in his claws a vanquished dragon. The eagle's wings support a large bookrack; a smaller rack, possibly for the use of choirboys, is attached below. Statuettes of Christ, saints, prophets, the Three Kings, and the Virgin and Child appear in the setting of mingled architecture and knotty branches.

It is believed that this lectern is the one that was confiscated and sold from the church of Saint Peter, in Louvain, in 1798, during the French occupation of Belgium.

In the church, as the big, or gospel, lectern, it would have stood to the left of the officiating priest, its polished surfaces gleaming.

Carolingian ivory plaque. Charlemagne, king of the Franks, was crowned Holy Roman Emperor in 800. The cultural revival he instigated, with its center initially in his palace at Aachen, is often called the Carolingian Renaissance. The revival spread to monastic centers in his realm, and it may have been in one of these where this ivory, once the front or back of a casket, was carved about 870. The intense and moving interplay of the figures, the sense of rounded bodies beneath the draperies, and the richness of the detail make this a superlative

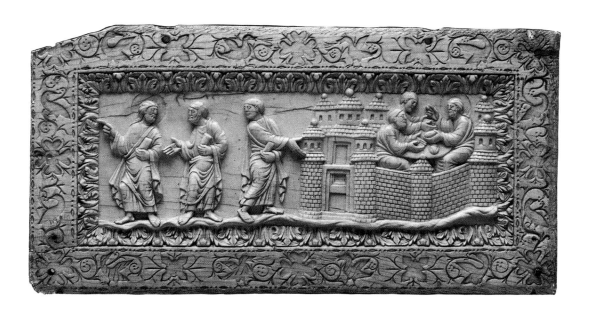

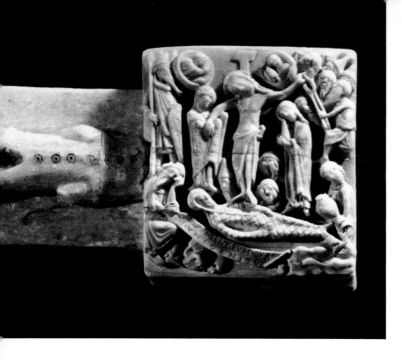

example of Carolingian art. At the left, Christ appears to two of his disciples after his Resurrection; at the right, we see the Supper at Emmaus. The representation of Emmaus—the carefully constructed gate, walls, and towers surrounding the figures—is a remarkable early achievement in suggesting three-dimensional space.

Cross of walrus-tusk ivory. Carved on both sides, this twelfth-century English Romanesque cross has on it more than a hundred small figures and some sixty inscriptions in Latin and Greek. Despite the complexity of the religious content—eight scenes from the Old Testament and the New, the allegory of the Lamb of God, likenesses of twenty-one prophets, and symbols of the Evangelists—the overall effect is one of simplicity and strength.

The cross is attributed to the abbey of Bury Saint Edmunds, Suffolk, England, by reason of its relationship to a Bible "incomparably painted" by Master Hugo for that abbey. It may even be the cross in the choir that Master Hugo is said to have made for Ording, who became abbot of Saint Edmunds in 1148.

Illuminated book: the Belles Heures. Books of hours were intended for the private devotions of the laity, their prayers to be said at the eight canonical hours of the day observed in monastic life. In medieval times such books were often richly illustrated. This one was made for Jean, duke of Berry, the same great patron and collector who owned the Nine Heroes Tapestries. The illuminators were Pol de Limbourg and his

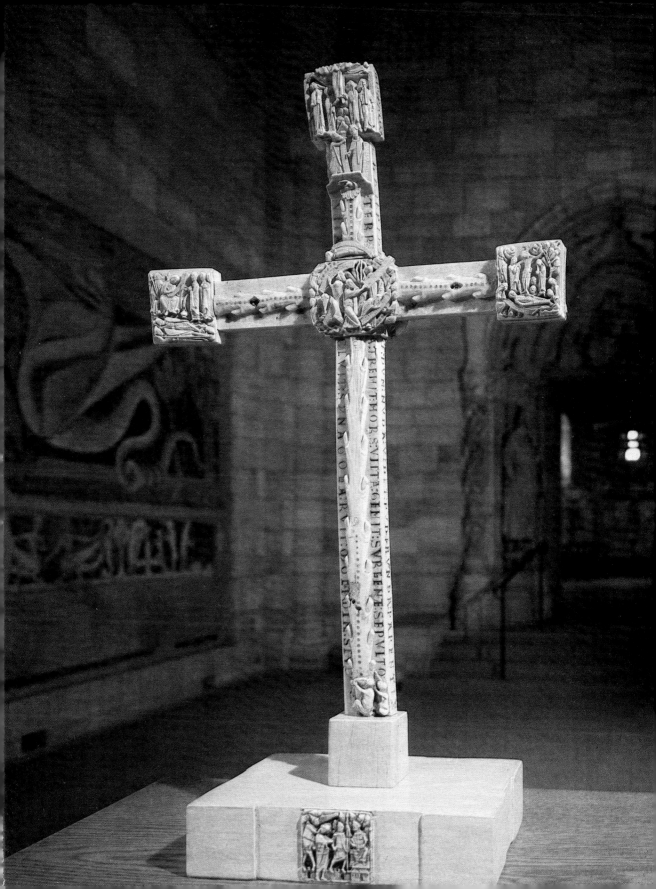

brothers Janequin and Herman; after working in Paris the three joined the duke's entourage and worked exclusively for him.

Since books went out of style less noticeably than more ostentatious objects, and since they could hardly be converted into bullion, they generally fared better than goldsmiths' work or jewelry. And they ordinarily suffered less damage than tapestries.

The exquisite paintings in this book, in tempera and gold, are nearly as fresh as they were in 1413, when it was recorded in the inventory of the duke's possessions as his "Belles Heures." The scene at the left, from the legend of Saint Eustace, shows his sons being abducted by a wolf and a lion. On the right, Saint Christopher carries the Christ Child across the dangerous stream.

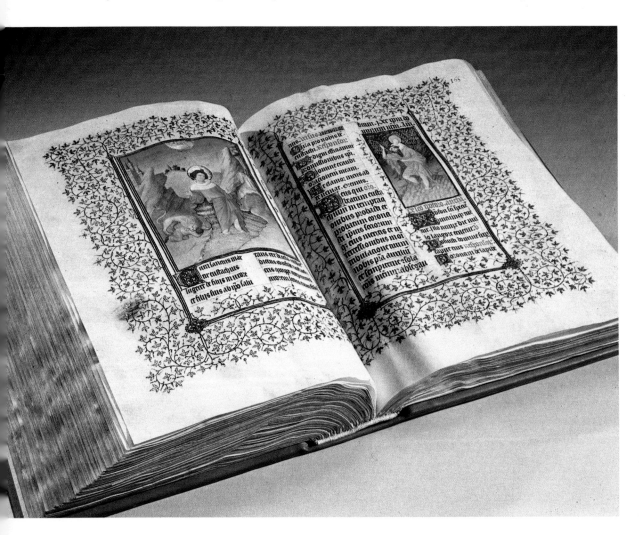

THE FROVILLE ARCADE

To conclude a walk through The Cloisters the visitor may wish to leave through this open-air corridor of fifteenth-century arches from the Benedictine priory of Froville, in Lorraine. The style here is late Gothic, showing pointed cusped arches grouped in threes, separated on the exterior by buttresses—originally this wall was one side of a small square cloister. It was the only side of the cloister to survive, the rest having been demolished before 1904 to make room for stables. Originally the walls of the cloister were plastered, and these arches may have been as well. It has been suggested that this is why toolmarks were left in the stone—so that the plaster would adhere. Whatever the reason, the marks now give the stone a rough, intriguing texture.

Arcades like these were popular in the fourteenth and fifteenth centuries, because they permitted solid construction but required neither great skill by the stonecutter nor great ingenuity by the designer.

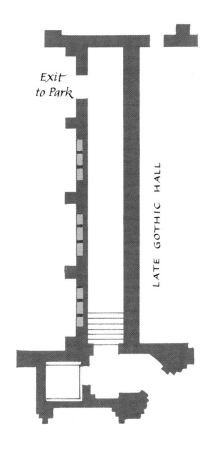

Exit
to Park

LATE GOTHIC HALL

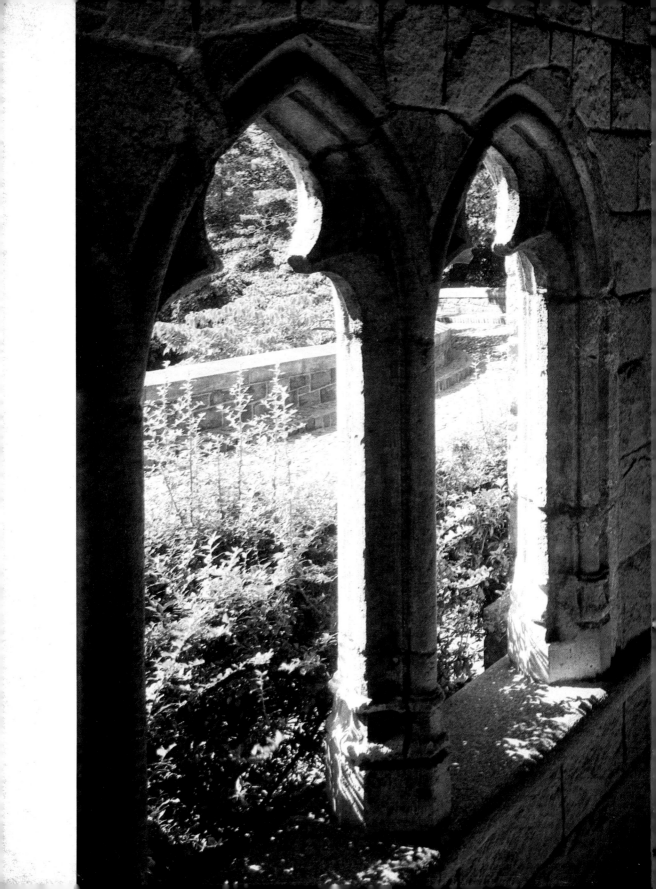

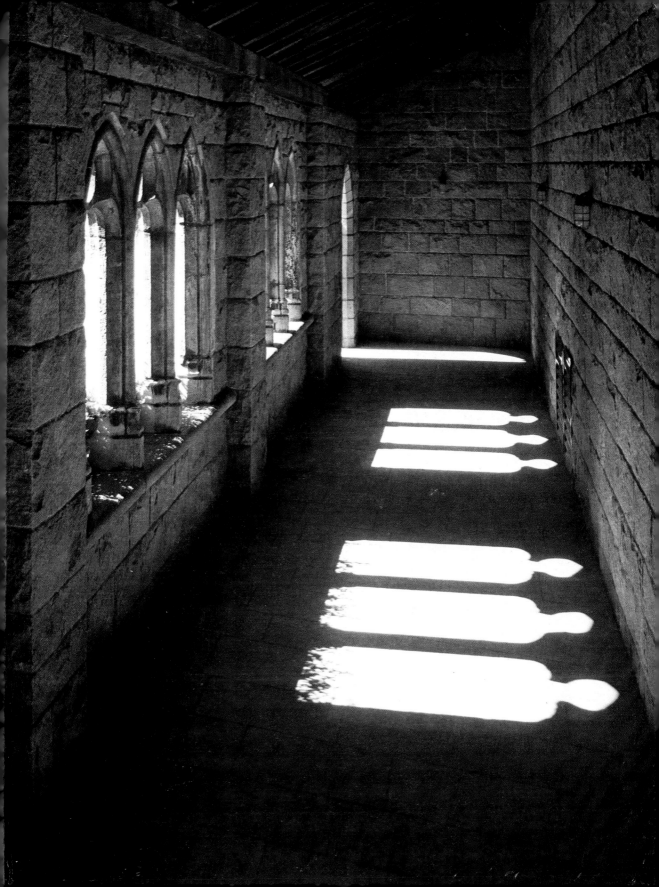

PUBLISHED BY
The Metropolitan Museum of Art, New York
Bradford D. Kelleher, Publisher
John P. O'Neill, Editor in Chief
Leon Wilson and Lauren Shakely, Editors
Peter Oldenburg, Designer

FLOOR PLANS BY
Joseph Ascherl

COMPOSED BY
Finn Typographic Service, Inc., Stamford, Connecticut

PRINTED BY
Mondadori Publishing Company, Inc., Verona, Italy

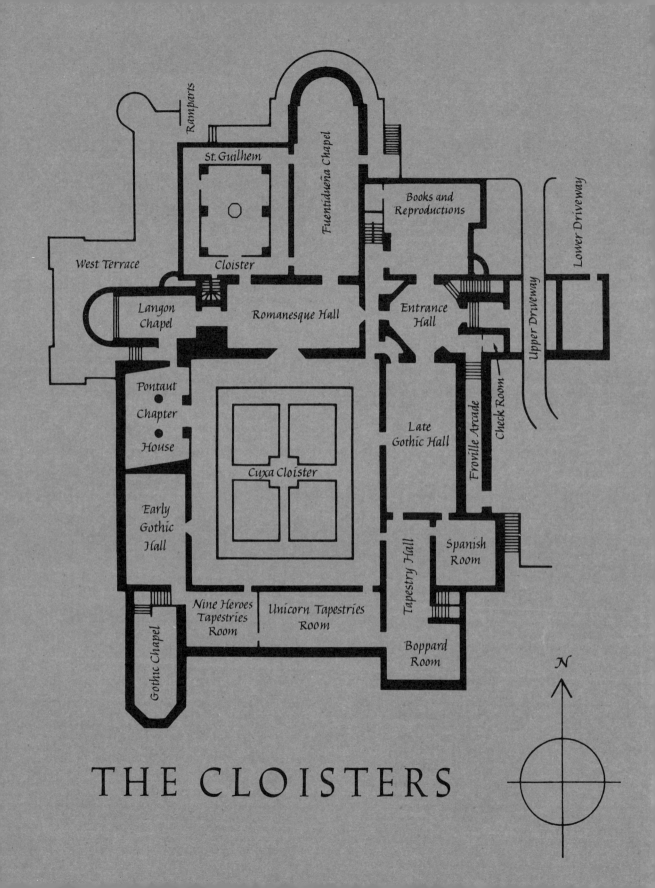

Ramparts

St. Guilhem

Fuentidueña Chapel

Books and
Reproductions

West Terrace

Cloister

Lower Driveway

Langon
Chapel

Romanesque Hall

Entrance
Hall

Upper Driveway

Pontaut

Chapter

House

Cuxa Cloister

Late
Gothic Hall

Froville Arcade

Check Room

Early
Gothic
Hall

Tapestry Hall

Spanish
Room

Gothic Chapel

Nine Heroes
Tapestries
Room

Unicorn Tapestries
Room

Boppard
Room

N

THE CLOISTERS